Baughman's
Handbook of Humor
in Education

Baughman's
Handbook of Humor
in Education

M. Dale Baughman

Parker Publishing Company, Inc.
West Nyack, New York

© 1974, *by*

PARKER PUBLISHING COMPANY, INC.
West Nyack, New York

Library of Congress Cataloging in Publication Data

Baughman, Millard Dale,
   Baughman's handbook of humor in education.

   Includes bibliographical references.
   1. Education--Anecdotes, facetiae, satire, etc.
I. Title. II. Title: Handbook of humor in educa-
tion.
LA23.B36   370'.2'07   74-11150
ISBN 0-13-072504-8

Printed in the United States of America

To the memory
of my father, Bert,
my mother, Josephine,
and my brother, Walter

                 and

To those yet with me
who are still growing—
my wife, D' Lema,
my daughters, Dala and Dlynn,
my son, Brad, and
my sister, Verna.

The Practical Value of
Humor in Education

Come laugh with me
For a span of brevity.
We'll enjoy some levity.

Your laugh and I must
Never part
For God and I love
A merry heart!

Come laugh with me.

—Nelda Porter in *Memphis Commercial Appeal*

King Amasis had a notorious routine. Every day he would get up at the crack of dawn and work like a Trojan the whole morning long. When the noon whistle blew, he stopped, pushed aside a heap of unsigned papers, punched the sundial and quit. He was through for the day. From then on there was little but fun and laughter as King Amasis gathered his cronies about him and they swapped funny stories.

But one day a friend took him aside and said, "Amasis, old scout, I hate to tell you this but the people are talking. They think a King should sit in state upon the royal throne and be a symbol of dignity." Amasis pondered that idea for a moment and then answered, "Listen, when an archer goes into battle, he strings his bow until it is taut; when the shooting is over, he unstrings it again. If he didn't, it would lose its snap and would be no good to him next time he needed it."

7

So unstring your bows now and then and come laugh with me. That's what this book is all about—jokes, jibes, ribs and rhyme in education.

Humor is a positive force in teaching and learning as well as in living. To you this is the kind of book that once you put it down, you know there'll be another occasion soon when you'll want to pick it up again. If it's laughter you're after, if you want to join in an effort to put a smile on the many faces of education, if you believe we can make happies out of hippies, this book will be like your checkbook after payday.

I've concluded after 32 years as an educator that most humor emanates from pupils and spreads among them. Having observed, visited, and supervised teachers at all grade levels, I must admit candidly it is a rare teacher who initiates humor and skillfully uses humorpower as a tool. Such a situation must not persist. This book can help you take a giant step toward greater effectiveness through teaching with humorpower.

Regardless of most other variables, the educator *does* make a difference. And those of us with humorpower make an even greater difference. This book will do several things for teachers and administrators who seek a higher humor quotient.

Section 1 describes and gives examples of many humor types. Section 2 explores some of the functions of humor which have been identified through research and clear thinking. It delves into the motivational qualities of humor, describing in a limited fashion relationships between humor and motives. You will find helpful ideas to enhance your understanding of just how important it is to use humor in thought and action.

Humor is explained as a tool for reducing aggression and releasing tensions and anxieties. In these days of teeny boppers, microboppers, emotional centaurs and members of the Pepsi generation, what pupils and teachers don't need that kind of help? Teachers and pupils are encouraged to laugh at themselves, thus acquiring a new kind of therapy from such self-directed humor.

Socialization has long been one function of education for adolescents and in Section 2 the author suggests how and why humor functions as a social lubricant. Teachers need to be armed with such knowledge so they may ease the social jolts of the "in betweeners." In today's hurry-up, pressure-packed, hot-house environment, which affects both children and teachers, a survival kit is needed. Humor can be a big item in that kit. Discover how.

But humor is also intellectual in nature. Properly and tactfully employed—and enjoyed—humor serves well as a cognitive challenge. Most educators know little of this phenomenon. Read about it and think about it.

Why employ humor? It can be an effective way to open and close class periods or "learning sessions" if you prefer. Preoccupied minds must be penetrated somehow.

Make this your "Good Humor" book and use its selections and ideas to increase and restore physical and mental tone in learners. Resort to humor when such distractions as the big game and forthcoming vacation periods play havoc with concentration and "heavy" work. Sometimes the best way to make your point is through the vehicle of humor. Lincoln used it, Charles Beard used it, and scores of great speakers use it. Why not you?

I could have stopped at the end of Section 2 but I didn't. Having been a hunter for many seasons, a hunter of humor, I have accumulated a vast amount of light-hearted and mirth-provoking material. I share with you in Section 3 more than 700 varied examples of humor which can be adapted to multiple uses in the education enterprise.

No apologies are made for the title and contents of this book. There's probably more supply than demand for the purely academic and thoroughly serious dimensions of the education enterprise. Resource materials which emphasize the lighter side of education are hard to find. We admit it. That's why we created this book.

M. Dale Baughman

ACKNOWLEDGEMENTS

I give thanks to the many friends and supporters who encouraged me along the path of humor and who thoughtfully donated to my bank of materials;

I appreciate the countless teachers, pupils and writers who create and/or express the healthful humor represented by this book;

I cherish the courage of the hundreds of program chairmen who invite me into their houses of learning to share with them my sense of the ludicrous;

I am grateful that three publications came into my life:

Quote, Anderson, South Carolina
Sunshine, Litchfield, Illinois
Comedy and Comment, 448 N. Mitchner Avenue, Indianapolis, Indiana

I am indebted to Rita, who attended to the mechanics of the manuscript.

Table of Contents

Baughman's
Handbook of Humor in Education

Types of Humor
and Applications
in Education

What's funny? Usually an answer to this question points to the individual respondent. Some clowns, some amusing incidents, some jokes are funny in and of themselves, yet when one hears a student or a teacher remark, "I think that's funny," or sees a person double up in laughter or even turn upward the corners of the mouth, he is observing individual responses.

There are many types of humor and it takes all of them sometimes to reach all pupils.

The Pun.

Words with same or similar sounds but with different meanings are used humorously for the express purpose of suggesting different meanings or applications. I do believe that puns may occur spontaneously or accidentally. At any rate there must be an infinite variety of puns.

Perhaps the earliest and most famous punster was Shakespeare, whose skillful use of puns included the nonsensical as well as the more profound. The late Bennett Cerf was considered to be the best known lover and transmitter of puns in his era.

Now, it's time to offer a pattern of punsmoke:

The situation is one where students frequent the soda fountain. One of them uses an effective technique of avoiding paying the check. It's called "shell-out falter."

17

Obviously the humor here requires that someone be familiar with the dangers of radioactive fall-out as well as the protective measures recommended. The rearrangement of syllables in "fall-out shelter" results in a type of humor.

Action stories appeal to many boys, especially if they refer to the adventures of flying an airplane. One pilot whose gasoline tank had been punctured in the bottom by a hunter's stray shot was forced to fly upside down to preserve his fuel supply. The tower radioed, "Loop before you leak." Such humor may bring a groan, a typical reaction to many puns. Nevertheless, there is an opportunity for pupils to use whatever creative talents they possess in converting proverbs and clichés to acceptable puns.

Broken water pipes in a home economics classroom damaged considerably the clothing materials which the girls had been cutting out for dresses. Quipped the teacher, "Too many brooks spoil the cloth." Both the quip and the humor are obvious, providing one has heard the expression from which the pun was formed.

A type of pun which features only a slight change in one word follows: A prospector had a pack animal which he used for double duty. The first is obvious. But each morning he listened for the animal to bray. One bray signalled a clear day, upon which the prospector set out to look for gold. Two brays indicated foul weather, so the prospector stayed in camp. He called the donkey his "weather burro." Surely such a play on words can serve to heighten the pupils' interest in words.

Although religion in the classroom is a moot point nowadays, the following pun-story can do no harm. A visitor to a new church was admiring the beautiful sanctuary, the spacious parlors and educational rooms. Eventually he inquired of the sexton, "Is your work ever done?" "Not really," he answered, "I have a hard enough time just minding my keys and pews."

As the perceptive learner will discern, pun lovers have a high regard for words and language. Maybe through punning, your apathetic students will acquire a greater appreciation of the English language. A new variety of the pun, called "fractured geography," is on the scene. The idea is to choose a town or city and define it in a most unlikely manner. What town in Pennsylvania gives you a ghostly feeling? Erie, what else?

The Limerick.

This particular form of humor is expressed in light verse form of five lines. Lines one, two and five consist of three feet and lines three and four are of two feet. The rhyme scheme is aabba. Limericks emphasize the peculiarities of the English language more than anything else known. This applies to spelling, pronunciation, and construction.

As the president of a Rotary Club, I have experienced the use of limericks as an approach to fellowship, fun and creativity. A bob-tailed limerick (one with line five missing) from *The Rotarian* was presented to the membership, who in turn could submit for judging their own last line. Winners were determined and rewarded. If Rotarians can use the limerick so effectively, just think what creative teachers can do with it!

Limericks appeal, possibly because they are short, because they tell an impossible event, because they twist words around, and because of the amusing rhymes. The limerick is popular with all kinds of people. Woodrow Wilson wrote limericks. Nearly everyone has a limerick he likes.

A light wit and a nimble tongue are all that many verses offer, and some not even that. Most limericks are perfectly ridiculous. They are nonsense rhymes. Whether they are nonsense rhymes at their worst or best, no one can say. A large portion of the known limericks are unfit for publication. Others have no merit. All that can be said for them is that they have the required five lines.

Some wit has remarked that there are really three kinds of limericks. The first are those you can tell to ladies. The second are those you can tell your preacher. The third are just limericks.

I think a fourth class might include those that should never be told to anyone!

One writer has said that a complete book of American limericks would be not only impossible, but also not at all desirable.

Some people hold that the only good limerick is a bad limerick.

When we think of absurd five-line verse, aabba, we think of the limerick. When we think of limericks we think of Edward Lear.

Given free choice of subject matter within the bounds of good taste, many pupils will create clever illustrations of great variety in their limericks. There it is—fun and learning at the same time.

You teach them and they don't know it's happening.

Comic Verse.

Not all light verse is in limerick form, of course, nor should it be. To require always that creative levity in verse be of limerick style would indeed be a straitjacket.

S. Omar Barker created this four-liner commentary on youth:

> You can tell it's adolescence
> Easily enough,
> When girls begin to powder
> And the boys begin to puff.

The new math has spread, illuminating the minds of kids but mystifying parents. Today advanced concepts are frequently introduced in the lowest grades, and Tony Antolini put it into verse:

> To be outdone by a computer
> Has always tied my mind in knots;
> But now they've got one even cuter:
> They're teaching calculus to tots!

Even the PTA appears in comic verse. One way is the Stephen Schlitzer way as first written in the *Nation's Schools:*

> Some return for a Ph.D,
> Others, perhaps, for their M.A.,
> Or maybe for some other degree,
> But most go back for the PTA.

Comic verse can be created and/or used in any subject field. In the U.S.A. we are sometimes criticized for the money and effort we spend on driver education. Yet Britain now has a spokesman who asks, "Why are safe driving knowledge and skills any less important than a knowledge of Shakespeare?"

> Two fools had cars they thought perfection.
> They met one day at an intersection,
> Tooted their horns and made a connection.
> A police car came and made a inspection.
> An ambulance came and made a collection.

> All that's left is a recollection—
> Two fewer voters in the next election.

Teachers themselves write humorously in verse about their own perplexities. Pupils might like to hear examples such as this one:

> There's satellites, rockets, and electrical sockets,
> New germs to uncover and stars to discover;
> A trip to the moon is enticing and might be;
> Living on Mars is entirely likely.
> Obsessed with the technical whirl they call progress,
> I'm literally batty but must not regress;
> Evolution, I love thee, but you're hard on the creatures
> Who keep up with your pace, the poor science teachers.

> —J.T., *Passing Marks*

The Gag.

Simply stated, the gag is any laugh-provoking remark or act. In our context we will deal only with remarks. Let it be clear—we are not talking about the kind of gag to prevent free speech or the kind designed to choke off any but guttural sounds.

The gag is brief, conversational and non-situational. As a humor type it is thought to have originated in vaudeville and minstrel shows.

"Why did you have such tough luck in your cooking class?" a doting aunt asked of her niece. "I flunked in defrosting," replied the teenager. Or this basic gag may be applied to another activity: "Why didn't you make cheerleader?" inquired a disappointed mother. An equally disappointed girl answered, "I flunked cartwheels."

The gag is often prevalent in the lives of academia also. A concerned father was describing his son to a close relative: "He's the serious, horn-rimmed glasses type—the kind who worries about the shortage of teachers." "Is he neurotic?" inquired the relative. "No, I won't say he's neurotic, but when he watches a football game and sees the teams go into a huddle, he wonders if they're talking about him."

There's plenty of room for teachers in "gag" humor too. Here's evidence: When a young attractive female teacher applied to the superintendent for a position, the employer asked, "How long do you plan to teach?" She replied in all candor, "From here to maternity."

The Joke.

When most people think of humor, they think first of jokes because so many are told and heard. Efforts to define the joke represent an exercise in futility. Perhaps a concept of the joke will suffice. In content it is longer than most elements of humor though generally shorter than an anecdote and usually without a serious point. The joke is built around a situation and typically devoid of dialogue.

If you're still interested in a definition, Webster writes: "A brief oral narrative with a climactic humorous twist." At any rate the joke is an element of humor which occupies a key position in the levity of life.

Here in successive order are jokes about an elementary teacher, a Latin teacher, and the PTA:

> The teacher was giving her class of third graders a lesson in association, and said to the class, "Now try to picture this scene. The man is on the river bank, and slips, falling into the river. While he is thrashing about in the water, his wife, hearing his screams and knowing that he can't swim, rushes to the bank. Now, why does she rush to the bank?" From the rear of the room, a tiny voice asked, "To draw out his insurance money?"
>
> A Latin teacher went into a drug store to look for a fountain pen. The clerk gave him one to try, and he wrote "Tempus Fugit" three times. The clerk watched him, then held out another pen and said, "Would you like to try this one, Mr. Fugit?"
>
> A housewife was honored recently by her PTA for her dedicated service. She was made a life member and given a pin. After the presentation, her husband asked to examine the pin. "I'd like to see what 2,000 TV dinners look like," he said wryly.

The joke writer or teller must focus on a single happening, avoiding superfluity and ambiguity. The surprise ending usually reverses an original assumption or perception.

Themes for jokes are multiple and varied and although the joke is a distinct element of humor, it is easily sub-divisible into singular types. In education those types might be the absent-minded professor joke, the tyrannical principal dilemma or nursery school nonsense.

The best joke writers tend to perceive the content of current events, those day-to-day happenings in society, or cyclical trends and then turn them into comic tales with situations and the unanticipated ridiculous climax. Jokes are born! Many times what results are different versions of a basic and older joke. Nevertheless the new variations are often amusing.

One last idea. The mere presence of a sudden reversal or an incongruity is not sufficient to produce laughter or even amusement. A joke is a medium for interaction. It must be told lightheartedly with intent to level and ease tensions. Most importantly it must establish contact in interaction among hearers.

The Anecdote.

Now we come face to face with a very useful humor tool for teachers and speakers. The anecdote is a short-to-medium length narrative of an interesting, amusing or biographical incident. More often than not a point or moral may be drawn from the narrative. My own name for these is "point stories." Some anecdotes describe certain aspects of the lives of well-known people. This type of anecdote may or may not have a moral or point.

For reasons perhaps best known to the composers and tellers of anecdotes, certain celebrities, politicians, statesmen and other colorful personalities have been the subject of dozens or even scores of anecdotal expressions. In any period of time anecdotes have tended to grow and bloom about specific individuals. As nearly everyone knows, Spiro Agnew, Jack Benny and Dean Martin are great subjects for anecdotes.

Even in the smallest of communities a certain small number of citizens seem to be the subject for anecdotes. I suspect that in your school district, in your classroom, or on your staff of teachers are pupils and teachers about whom anecdotes are easy to build. Certainly many principals, superintendents and janitors are frequently described through the use of anecdotes. As long as they are healthy and supportive of good mental health, they can be a good source of humor both to teller and listener.

Not just in English or in creative writing classes but also in such other classes as art, music and history can the creative and humorous teacher discover ways to involve pupils in writing, telling, hearing and responding to anecdotes.

Here is a good anecdote about positive thinking. It concerns General Creighton Abrams, Commander in Vietnam.

> During World War II Abrams commanded the Fourth Armored Division, a unit of Patton's third army, and dashed across France in a tank named "Thunderbolt."
>
> It was Abrams who raised the seige of Bastogne and rescued General Tony McAuliffe, the man who told the Germans "Nuts!"
>
> On one occasion, Abrams found his outfit surrounded by Germans. The Nazi commander sent the usual demand for surrender. Abrams sent the usual refusal, then called his men together. "Gentlemen," he boomed. "We are today faced with a great opportunity. For the first time in this campaign we can attack the enemy in every direction."
>
> And that is what is called positive thinking.

While the above anecdote may not create laughter, it does tend to amuse to some extent and relate to the work of the educator.

The perceptive humorist or for that matter an aspiring teacher-humorist will be able to extend and enlarge many jokes into anecdotes. Teachers frequently need to make a point in a dramatic fashion. It can be done—and is being done every day somewhere by teachers who use the anecdote in a brief, lively and amusing way.

Rustic Humor.

In the early 1900's Franklin McKinney "Kin" Hubbard created a cartoon character, Abe Martin, through whom he expressed his humor. Abe was a single-gallused cracker barrel "philosofuner" with a floppy hat supposed to be living in Brown County, Indiana. The Abe Martin sayings accompanying each cartoon were of the country or village variety and appeared in the *Indianapolis News* for many years. Now, years after Kin Hubbard's death, the best ones are being re-run.

When he created Abe Martin, Hubbard found a good formula for producing a brand of humor leading to the chuckle; people don't tend to laugh uproariously at Hubbard humor. His formula was to report a human situation with sharp accuracy. "A keen enough observer," he said, "can report on what happened at a tea party or a PTA meeting with amusing effects."

Among Abe Martin sayings were these:

> "I don't think much of a dance where the girl looks like she wuz bein' carried out of a burnin' buildin'."
>
> "A boy pianist never puts on long pants 'til he's 40 years old."
>
> "You never get what you want fer Christmas after you grow up."
>
> "We like children 'cause they tear out as soon as they get what they want."
>
> "I hate eatin' by a feller that holds his arms like a snare drummer."
>
> "The louder a feller laughs at nothin' th' more popular he is."
>
> "Classic music is th' kind we keep thinkin' will turn into a tune."

Rustic humor holds some appeal for city and suburban youth, especially if they have enough understanding of the rural way of life. Whether or not such humor appeals to rural youth depends a great deal on how they regard or value their situations in life. If they are positive about and satisfied with the rural way, it's likely that their response to humor directed at aspects of their own lives will be wholesome. On the other hand, those young people who resent their rustic environment and envy the more sophisticated city dwellers are likely to find no therapy, support or joy in rustic humor.

City youth frequently are late to school for a variety of reasons—"missed the city bus," "got railroaded," "became embroiled in a gang fight on the way," etc. The following incident clearly and ludicrously pictures how a rural youth might be detained and thus destined to arrive late at school:

> It seems that this boy showed up late for school. The teacher asked him for an explanation and he said, "Well, I guess you could say it's because pa sleeps in his shorts." "What's that got to do with your being late?" the teacher snapped. "It's like this, ma'am," the boy replied. "You see, last night we heard a noise in the chicken house. Pa jumped out of bed, wearing his shorts, and grabbed his shotgun. He ran out to the chicken house, opened the

door and pointed the gun inside. About that time our old dog,
Rover, come up behind pa and sniffed pa's bare laig. Well, ma'am,
we been cleanin' chickens since 3 o'oclock this morning."

One-liners.

Naturally, I advocate a laughing place and time for every
teacher and pupil. Some writers try to make people ponder, or
cry, or fear, and I'm quite sure that these are respectable goals.

The one-liner or the quip is an extrememly brief commentary
on almost anything which induces amusement, joy and/or laughter. Now and then, I must admit, some of mine bring only groans.

Examples which follow suggest the characteristics of quips or
one-liners:

> "Teaching junior high school youth with high school and
> college lecture methods is like trying to waltz to rock and roll
> music."

> "How do history teachers keep a straight face when they tell
> students the early settlers came to America to escape high taxes?"

> "It's unbelievable but true that the average school teacher
> makes more money in a year than a professional athlete makes in
> a whole week."

> "Nowadays the voice crying in the wilderness is just a
> teen-ager with a transistor."
>
> (*–Changing Times*)

> "Did you hear about the teen-ager who plans to run away
> from home just as soon as she gets a long enough telephone
> extension cord?"

> "Anyone who thinks the younger generation isn't creative
> should watch a teen-ager build a sandwich."
>
> (A.W. Eiselin, *Wall Street Journal*)

> "The little boy used to help old people across the street is now
> chasing them across with his car."
>
> (–F.G. Kernan, *Link* Vol. 20, No. 6)

> "Class reunion–where people get together to see who's falling
> apart."

Riddles.

Sometimes humorous, sometimes not, the riddle is a mystifying, misleading or puzzling question posed as a problem to be solved or guessed. At one time the riddle represented the highest form of humor to juveniles. Without doubt it has lost some of its appeal to all but the very young, those we choose to call pre-adolescent.

As a form of humor the riddle has great potential in developing creative writing as well as creative guessing. Naturally, a creative teacher must be the catalyst.

Teachers who are convinced that too many pupils have been resting their brains might say "Exercise that brain by solving these oldies:"

> 1. What is the best way for an instructor to teach bookkeeping? 2. When do elephants have eight feet? 3. What are the wrinkles in a merchant's forehead? 4. What did the right eye say to the left? 5. Which of the stars should be subject to the game laws? 6. What is the worst age to live in? 7. What is light as a feather, yet a thousand men can't lift it? 8. How much is one and a half dozen? 9. Why is the sun like a loaf of good bread? 10. If a car can run over a dog, what would stop a wagon?
>
> *Answers:* 1. By telling the students, "Never lend them." 2. When there are two elephants. 3. Trademarks. 4. "There's something between us that smells." 5. Shooting stars. 6. Bondage. 7. A bubble. 8. Seven. 9. It is light when it rises. 10. The dog's tail would stop a-waggin'.

Riddles are mind stimulators to start the wheels rolling again. The wise teacher knows that vacation periods, three-day weekends, special holidays and the ordinary two-day weekend are periods when some intellectual wheels do come to rest. What better way to start the action again than with these sets of riddles?

> 1. What did one candle say to another candle? 2. What book is not for reading? 3. Why is an empty purse always the same? 4. What roads are bad tempered? 5. Which is the laziest mountain in the world? 6. What do you have if you drop a letter in the mud? 7. Why is a calendar sad? 8. If you saw a girl with the heel of her shoe coming off, what would be her name? 9. What is an eavesdropper? 10. What do bees do with their honey?

Answers: 1. "Going out tonight?" 2. A pocketbook. 3. Because you see no change in it. 4. Crossroads. 5. Everest. 6. Blackmail. 7. Its days are numbered. 8. Lucille. 9. An icicle. 10. They cell it.

Boners.

To be perfectly candid and extra brief, a boner is a blunder. Although no one in school, including administrators, teachers and custodians, has a natural immunity to them, boners are amusing and gross errors usually made by students at any and all levels in reply to oral or written questions.

While it is true that the production of boners is not equally distributed among school subjects, a keen observer will find them in any part of the school curriculum. They are commonly spawned by the substitution of one word for another of similar sound, confusion of ideas, illogical reasoning, and unintentional word-play.

These examples which follow may remind the teacher of others or at least signal her to be on the lookout for more. Boners are plentiful and often beautiful if not always flattering.

> A teacher was giving a talk about kindness to animals. "If I saw a boy beating a donkey and made him stop, what virtue would I be showing?" "Brotherly love," quickly replied the impulsive pupil.
>
> A famed zoologist came to talk to a group of ninth graders about the danger of rat infestation. The young people listened attentively, then when the lecture was over, one girl rose to speak the class' thanks. She ended by saying, "We didn't even know what a rat looked like until you came to our school."

The Tongue Twister

Difficulty in articulating a series of words or sentences is the essence of the humor of tongue twisters. Both the talker and the listener may enjoy the outcome, the former deriving his pleasure from the ludicrous challenge and the latter from hearing the usual futile attempts which likely turn out to be sounds and/or words not originally intended.

Let your pupils give their tongues a twist and a turn by having them read aloud and swiftly these gems:

> Twisting and turning, the twenty-two trampers tried to tra-
> verse the twelve ridges.
> Wally walked through the wood where the wagtails warbled.
> I want two dozen double damask dinner napkins.
> Saturday's coal stocks soared.

The following twisters should be practiced several times in private before any public utterances:

> Two toads totally tired, tried to trot to Trettertown.
> The swans swam over the silvery sea; swim swans, swim; the
> swans swam back again; swans swim well.
> Six thick thistle sticks.
> Strict, strong Stephen Stringer snares six sickly silky snakes.
> Give Grimes Jim's gift gilt whip.
> Simple Susan shineth shoes and socks; socks and shoes shineth
> simple Susan. She ceaseth shining shoes and socks, for shoes
> and socks shock simple Susan.
> A haddock, a haddock, a black spotted haddock, a black spot on
> the black back of a black spotted haddock.

Delivered by very limber and nimble tongues, this group of twisters should draw a laugh or two from nearly any company of people:

> Three thrifty tinkering tailors totally tired.
> Samuel Short's sister Susan sat sewing silently.
> Sweet, sagacious Sallie Sanders said she sure saw seven segregated
> seaplanes sailing swiftly southward Saturday.
> Two tall Turks twirled turbans tastefully.

Since Jimmy was more or less unsuccessful in pronouncing the letter "R," his teacher gave him this sentence to practice on. "Robert gave Richard a rap in the ribs for roasting the rabbit so rare."

A few days later the teacher asked him to say the sentence for her. Said Jimmy, "Bob gave Dick a poke in the side for not cooking the bunny enough."

The above incident suggests one practical use of the tongue twister. In treating specific speech defects it has been of great value. Speech teachers use material for improving diction, a second useful employment of this so-called element of humor. In preliminary try-outs, radio and TV announcers are typically asked to recite some of the most challenging twisters.

After I had delivered more than a dozen addresses during an eight-week span in Wisconsin, operating from my base at the University of Illinois, Champaign, I was christened "The Hurryin' Hoosier Humorist." Since that time many a program chairman in introducing me has stumbled over that one.

Publication Bloopers.

Amusement is often found among the many millions of words printed in newspapers, magazines, newsletters, bulletins and books annually. With the theory of probability at work bloopers are there, just waiting to be found and woven into some kind of humor pattern.

School officials must have cringed when they read in *The Daily Argus,* Mt. Vernon, New York, these famous last words: "The fall term will begin with clashes in the first through fourth grades inclusive."

In view of today's secondary school problems in human relations the above announcement would have been more prophetic than humorous had it referred to junior or senior high school grades.

School papers are, believe it or not, not much more guilty of bloopers than are commercial publications. Here's an exception, however, in a news item from a Virginia school paper:

> "Mr. Brown visited the school yesterday and lectured on destructive pests. A large number were present."

Whoever wrote copy for the following announcement didn't really mean it but here's what readers read:

> "Plan to eat dinner on October 16 with the Band Parents in the school cafeteria. The same wonderful dinner as served last year."

Although the following blooper appeared in the "Situations Wanted" column of a daily paper, it isn't really an error by the paper but rather an inexcusable blunder by the writer of the ad:

"If you are not satisfied with your child's progress at school, why not have he or she tutored at home by an experienced teacher?"

(E.E. Kenyon, *American Weekly, Quote*)

A new service in apartment living? According to an ad in a Texas newspaper, it appeared so:

"Spring Branch. New deluxe air-conditioned apartments. Near elementary and high school. Children welcome. Also furnished."

Really now!

Fun with Words.

During a vocabulary lesson in prefixes, the teacher explained, "One prefix we often use is 'trans.' It means 'across,' and we use it in words like 'transatlantic.' " She looked around the room and then asked, "Now can any of you think of other words that use the same prefix?"

A little boy raised his hand.

"Yes, Tommy," smiled the teacher.

"How about 'transparent,' " volunteered the child, "meaning 'a cross parent'?"

(*Quote:* 11/5/72)

While we may find some humor in the above, it's unlikely that foreigners find much to laugh at in the learning stages at least. All wordplay, though, doesn't hinge on multiple meanings of words.

"A gas container was placed upside down and a candle inserted. When it was in it was out, and when it was out it was in." Pupils might enjoy the humor in these words while they are experimenting or watching a demonstration.

Many high school teachers find themselves with unruly classes. A sense of humor helps. One teacher, upon entering his classroom and finding it in a state of bedlam, plopped his hand on the desk with a loud clap and shouted, "I demand pandemonium." Pupils are likely to sense the humor and respond more positively than they might to a demand for quiet.

A New Jersey teacher after considerable experience in interaction with his pupils reached these conclusions:

1. It is the teachers that will be taut.
2. Nothing succeeds like recess.
3. At the end of the day his grief case is full.

Our new educational technology is responsible for this "word" humor. "Did you hear about the young teacher who thought an individual carrel was a Christmas solo?"

A Glenwood, Iowa, teacher was laying down the law on the subject of behavior in study hall. After citing several rules, she concluded, "You may be excused to leave the room if it's absolutely necessary but only one at a time. I don't want a steady stream in the hall."

Typically, fun with words is to be found in the utterings and writings of pupils. Some is accidental, some is intentional, and that last word leads us to our next example of wordplay:

> An eight-year old absentee explained at school recently why she'd been absent: "I came down," she announced, "with intentional flu."
>
> Rom Tyers, one of my high school classmates, occasionally took a day off from school to go rabbit hunting. He always signed his absence blank with the excuse, "Taking shots."

If pupils can be absent from school with "intentional flu" and for "taking shots," there must be dozens of other such excuses as yet unexpressed by anyone. There is fun in words! One day Tommy skipped school to go fishing. He didn't catch a thing—until he got home.

To some pupils words are complex, especially when they are to be used in proper context. It's quite common to use the wrong word now and then.

> First day at school, teacher asked each pupil to give a short talk about his pet. After a detailed account of all the tricks his dog could do, Johnny sat down. "What kind of a dog is he?" asked teacher. "Well, he's a mixed-up kind," the boy answered. "Sort of a cocker scandal."

Sometimes though, the humor results from the pupil's knowledge rather than his ignorance of a word as witnessed in this situation:

> There was a school teacher once who had a big fellow in her class whom she considered rather dumb, and as they were talking about ignorance she asked him, "What is the meaning of gross ignorance?" He rose to his feet, scratched his head and said, "Ma'am, gross ignorance is 144 times plain ignorance."

> A man told a pullman agent that he wanted a pullman berth. "Upper or lower?" the agent asked. "What's the difference?" the man made the mistake of asking. "One dollar," said the agent. "The lower is higher than the upper. The higher price is for the lower. If you want a lower price you have to go higher. We sell the upper lower than the lower. Most people don't like the upper because it's higher and you have to get up to go to bed and get down to get up. The lower is higher. If you are willing to go higher, the price will be lower."

Life among the acronyms is often amusing. An acronym is a linguistic mutation which has flourished unchecked since World War II. It is simply a new name made up of the first letters of several words. Examples: WAVES (Women's Appointed Volunteer Army Corps), HELP (Housewives Effort for Local Progress).

> When the principal of an elementary school began publishing a monthly staff newsletter, he asked for suggestions for a name for the bulletin. The first suggestion was FACULTY—for "Frantic Adults Chasing Unruly Little Tireless Youngsters."

A somewhat more recent arrival to this category of humor is the "prankish preposition," the following examples of which came out of newspapers:

> "The girl was stabbed in the suburbs."
> "Local man-about-town shot in his Chrysler."
> "She walked in upon his invitation."
> "She fainted upon her departure."

As anyone can see the "Fun with Words" category of humor is both extensive and expansive. New directions are common. Here truly is an area where imaginative and humor-oriented teachers can teach much about words in a fun setting.

Report Card Day Shock.

This is a phenomenon of American life which usually perpetrates more anguish than humor. Some research has turned up such evidence as run-aways, attempted suicides, divorces, parental dissension—all over the shock wave of that report card. How could anything so obviously devastating in its effects have even a shred of humor about it? Well, it does.

For some strange reason the object of the humor is "good" or "bad" for old dad as these first two examples attest:

> "Here," said Johnny to his father, "is my report card. And here," he added triumphantly, " is an old one of yours I found."
> Mother: "Have you scolded Willie for the low marks on his report card?" Father: "No. Every time I try, he reminds me he's an exemption on my income tax."

In other "shock day" situations the resulting humor can be traced to the creativity of the youngsters:

> Little Johnny asked his father,"Dad, can you sign your name with your eyes closed?" "I don't know," replied dad. "I never tried. Why do you ask?" "I wanted you to sign my report card," answered the child.

Think about it. What better way to spend part of a period the day after report cards reach the parents than to have a "sharing" session wherein volunteers describe humorous episodes surrounding the evaluation received. After all, if there can't be some humor, something to laugh about, maybe those report cards just aren't worth it.

Seasonal and Holiday Humor.

Having been a humor buff since year 1 (meaning my first teaching year back in 1939) I can assure you that there is r-o-o-o-m for humor in this broad category. Everybody is involved—teachers, parents, principals, pupils. When you think of seasons, think of the usual ones, plus the vacation ones, the melancholy ones, the tax ones. Who said kids can't produce humor?

> The ABC Bulletin relates the story of the pupil whose teacher asked him to "name two documents that have contributed heavily to our government." Obviously a good listener at home, the boy replied: "Forms 1040 and 1040A."
>
> When the fourth grader was asked which he liked the best— winter or summer—he was positive about summer. When pressed for his reason he said: "Well, in winter there is school and you've got to be a-thinking about a-doing, but in summer all you have to be is a-doing!"

Dad too is involved somehow in the seasonal nature of the lives of his offspring and while it's dead serious to him, there's humor in it if one is willing to accept it.

> From a contributor: "When the frost is on the pumpkin and the fodder's in the shock, dad buys his children's school books and finds himself in hock."

Holidays, along with the joys and cheer, the fun and the frustrations they provide, offer multiple opportunities for humor to flourish. Since there are so many holidays to represent in a humorous way, I am limiting examples here to Christmas. And in no way do I intend anything sacrilegious. I know, understand and appreciate its real meaning.

> A Minneapolis family, like all of us, is being deluged currently with gift catalogs from all the stores. This gave the three-year-old an inspiration. During a discussion about what to give daddy for Christmas, she announced: "I know what I'll get him—a toy catalog."
>
> A Minneapolis six-year-old has been blabbing that there isn't any Santa Claus. The other day he asked mom and dad to take him downtown to see that jolly gentleman. "I thought you didn't believe in Santa Claus," they said. "I believe in toys," he said.
>
> Ad in the Green Bay, Wisconsin, *Press-Gazette*: " 'Twas the night before Christmas, and all through the house, not a creature was stirring, not even a mouse.'—Canadeo Exterminating Company."

Anticipation and expectation are at the core of Christmas emotions for children but there is always an aftermath which typically leaves parents in various states of regret. Yet humor does prevail. Here's some:

> 'Tis the day after Christmas and inside and out, the holiday mess lies scattered about. And ma with a wet towel atop of her head and aspirin tablets has crawled into bed. The kiddies, God bless 'em, are raising a din, with thundering drums and shrill trumpets of tin. While pa, like a schoolboy, forgetting his years, is all tangled up in the bicycle gears.
>
> Old Duffer, the dachshund, delightfully smug, lies gnawing a carcass upon the new rug. And Muffet, the kitten, despaired of a lap, on the dining room table is taking her nap. Plaid neckties and pink socks and what-nots galore await their exchange at the five-and-ten store. While tidbits and knickknacks of leftover sweets must furnish the menu for future-day eats.
>
> 'Tis the day after Christmas, and once every year folks willingly pay for their holiday cheer. With toothaches from candy and headaches from bills, they call up the doctor and order more pills.
>
> Mama insists that what the country needs is a do-it-yourself Christmas tree. One that will gather up all the litter, take it with itself and vanish.

Communications Humor.

Misunderstanding on someone's part is the keystone of most humorous effects observed in communications involving schools and their articulating elements.

Perhaps more often than not it's the pupil who doesn't interpret the message as it was intended.

> Little Mary stood red-nosed and covered with snow while her teacher struggled to unfasten her overshoes for her. "Did your mother hook these for you?" the teacher asked. "No," the child answered. "She bought 'em at J.C. Penneys."

In the communication process a message is encoded and transmitted by the sender; then a receiver decodes the message—and as every thoughtful person knows many messages are decoded differently from what the encoder had in mind.

Sometimes when we're dealing with keen minds and playful minds we can't be sure why the impasse and accompanying humor occurred. It may be misunderstanding and it just may be premeditated. In the following two situations judge for yourself:

> At Denby High School in Detroit, a teen-age student recently asked her tenth-grade English teacher if she could read "that new dance book" for her regular Friday book report. The teacher, having assigned the class a list of classics, was somewhat puzzled. "You know," the girl replied brightly, "Oliver Twist."
>
> A small Republican boy was asked by his teacher, "What is the size of the Democratic Party?" "About five feet two inches," he promptly replied. "Idiot!" exploded the teacher. "I mean how many members does it have? How do you get five feet two inches?" "Well," replied the boy, "my father is six feet tall and every night he puts his hand to his chin and says, 'I've had the Democratic Party up to here!'"

Now and then it happens. The teacher is the one whose decoding creates the humor. Religion in the school being a controversial topic, the teacher in the incident following must have felt real relief:

> Some pupils were busily engaged on their knees on the floor in the back of the classroom. The teacher entered and asked, "What are you doing?" One little fellow explained, "We're shooting craps." "Thank heavens!" retorted the teacher. "For a moment I thought you were praying."

There's one sure thing about a first year teacher's experiences. Anything can happen and usually does. Who could have predicted what happened in the story which follows? Yes, it's anticipate or acquiesce.

> It was my first day as a teacher. I entered the classroom to find a mischievous-looking class facing me. So I made it a point to be very firm about the kind of work I expected from them. I ended my speech by saying that it would take more than just an "apple for the teacher" to earn a passing mark.
>
> Apparently I made my point, for on the following morning a pupil presented me with a watermelon.
>
> —Mrs. B.R. Setm, *Rotarian*

The scope of educational humor is so great that the more a person thinks about it the more possibilities come to mind. Actually in this category of communications humor there is a rather significant sub-category which might be called "school-to-home and home-to-school" humor.

In the first instance which follows a teacher reveals a high humor quotient:

> One teacher exercised both wit and wisdom in dealing with parents when she penned this note: "If you promise not to believe everything your child says happens at school, I'll promise not to believe everything he says happens at home."

Not all classroom howlers and humorous incidents are written or created by pupils and teachers, however. Hurriedly or poorly written notes from parents constitute a fertile source of school humor:

> In a school in one of the poorer districts of a big city, a questionnaire was sent home with a new pupil requesting information regarding the home environment, number of brothers and sisters, father's occupation and so on. The next day the child returned with a scrap of paper on which was written, "We have 18 children. My husband can also do plumbing and carpentry work."

> "Please do something about Johnny before I do. I think it is those comic books he is always reading. Yesterday I asked him what was the distance from the schoolhouse to his home and he wanted to know if I wanted the answer in light years. Does he by any chance take after his father?"

> The teacher added a note to Johnny's report card. "Johnny's not contributing!" Next day Johnny came to school with a scrawled note which read, "We don't have much money but here's a nickel."

> A schoolteacher wrote to the mother of a pupil: "William was absent this morning. Will you please tell me what kept him out?" "Dear Ma'am," was the reply; "Willie is keeping time for his father. Last night he came home with an example about how long would it take a man walking three miles an hour to walk two-and-one-half times around a field four miles square. And as Willie ain't no man, we had to send his pap. They left erly this morning but I don't know when they will git back. Please make

the next problem about something else, as my husband hasn't the time for such things."

Gertrude Sonner of Durfee School, Detroit, cited these examples as typical of many notes she has received from parents:

"I'm sorry you called and couldn't get us. The kids had the flu but are fine now. Our telephone is permanently disconnected. Hope this finds you the same."

"Don't let Betty buy candy for lunch. Doctor says she is too fat. He wants to seduce her."

"As you can see, Tom has his arm tied up. If he feels bad, let him put his head on the desk because he broke it."

Teacher Dilemmas.

According to Nathan Nielsen teachers have tough problems. One moment they're told to worry about too many overcrowded schools, and in the next breath they're told to worry about too many dropouts.

There's a story going around about a little kid in Bloomington, Illinois, so tough the teacher keeps bringing him apples.

One naive teacher asked a pupil to explain what a hypocrite is. He replied, "It's a boy who comes to school with a smile on his face."

After a trying day, a young teacher was filling out a school health questionnaire. She pondered the question, "Have you ever had a nervous breakdown?" then wrote; "Not yet, but watch this space for further developments."

Adolescent Dilemmas.

Adolescents are special people with special problems. Often referred to as "emotional centaurs," "marginal people," "tweeners," the "here and now age" or "members of the Pepsi generation," they frequently find themselves in dilemmas which, though serious to them, produce humorous reactions in others. Today's adolescent knows there is no velvet-lined path to adulthood. He is confused and no wonder. According to Charlie Wadsworth, half the adults tell him to find himself and the other half tell him to get lost.

Heterosexual interests are prominent in this age group, but as one observer candidly put it, the age of chivalry is not yet dead. If a teen-ager girl drops her book, somewhere is a teen-age boy who will kick it back to her (—Hobart, N.Y. *Rotary Howl*).

Other analysts of the adolescent subculture say that the best way to keep teen-agers at home is to make home pleasant—and one good way to do that is let each one have his own phone and 50 feet of extension cord. Another way to keep them home is to let the air out of the tires.

The following story describes one of many dilemmas into which youth often stumble headlong.

> The romantic adolescent school girl raced up the stairs after having been excused from the table. Closing the door behind her she made a dive for the book she had concealed from the prying eyes of her family. She'd purchased it from a second-hand dealer just before making a dash for the bus and hadn't had a chance to open it until now. One more look at its heartthrobbing title, "How to Hug" and then with trembling hand she opened the cover—only to find she'd bought the sixth volume of an out-of-print encyclopedia, defining words beginning with "How" through those beginning with "Hug."

More humor on adolescents will be found under the appropriate heading in the third section of the book.

Kindergarten Kapers.

When timid kindergarteners reluctantly let go of mommy's hand and encounter that first rung of our educational ladder, the possibilities for humor mushroom. Generally the fun grows out of their various perceptions of the world as they learned to know it in their pre-kindergarten years. Naturally, it's a giant step for the child who sometimes finds his ego quite enlarged. Parents know it too.

> "Is the head of the house at home," inquired a salesman of the lady who answered the door. "No," she replied, "he's in kindergarten right now."
>
> (*—Comedy and Comments*)
>
> Anxious to show the school supervisor how alert were the kids in her kindergarten class, a young teacher slapped a half-dollar

down on her desk and demanded, "What is it?" A boy in the front row shouted, "Tails!"

Even at this early age the wit of the neophyte pupil expresses itself. Jackie Allen, a kindergartener, returned home and was asked by his daddy, "Did you learn anything today?" "No," replied the kid, "but I didn't forget anything."
(—Mickey Porter, *Akron Beacon Journal, Comedy and Comment*)

The very real difference between memorized learning and functional learning is brought to the fore in this little vignette:

The kindergartener rushed into the house and proudly told her mother, "Guess what, mommy! I learned to say, 'Yes, ma'am.' and 'No, ma'am,' in school today." "Did you really?" responded the mother. "Yeah."

Student Masterpieces.

Both spontaneous and assigned writings of pupils provide a mountain of mirth. The laughable elements of the essays and themes are sometimes the products of clever minds and sometimes nothing more than carelessness or weak word usage. An example of the first type is the following brief passage:

A small boy approached the librarian and asked, "Do you have anything on the parent from 30 to 35?" He found something, and being a precocious youngster wrote, "It is useless to try to change most adults. Studies of many cases show that this can rarely be done, even by others. However, life can be made much happier for everybody if we understand that most adult behavior, however odd it may seem, is normal for that age and that they are going to behave that way anyway."

Perhaps a classic example of the second type of masterpiece appears in this portion of a narrative:

An English teacher in St. Paul, Minnesota, reports that one of his students, in telling the story of a fire, wrote: "Trying to save Alice, I ran from the door, dragging her behind. ...By the time our parents got home, our house was totally diminished."

In Discussing the problem of mental health, one boy wrote, "Too many people get drove crazy. One reason is their nerves."

A small girl wrote the following composition on men: "Men are what women marry. They drink and smoke and swear, but don't go to church. They are more logical than women and also more zoological. Both men and women sprung from monkeys, but the women sprung further than the men."

Not all strange things are in print, of course. From Santa Barbara, California, Caroline Hennings reports that she asked a class, "In what verse form are Shakespeare's plays written?" One answer: Dynamic pentameter.

Some teachers find it completely impossible to stay in a rut. They invent, modify and create learning experiences for children which afford releases from tension and hum-drum.

Mrs. Pansye Powell last spring asked her fourth period creative writing class at Abington, Pennsylvania, High School to twist some quotes for practice. Here are some the boys and girls came up with: Home is where the car isn't. . . . Where there's a will, there's a way to break it. . . .How do I love thee? Let me count the dollars. . . . Believing is seeing it the teacher's way.

Examination Humor.

Closely related to student masterpiece humor, though different in that responses are made under pressure, is a brand of school humor I choose to call exam humor.

The incongruities in word usage in the "shorties" which follow provide a chuckle, a grin or a laugh, depending on the reader's perceptions:

A sixth grader wrote in an exam paper: "It was Nathan Haley who said, 'I regret that I have but one life to lose for my country.' This has come to be known as Haley's Comment."

Little Sally was determined to give her hero full credit for his achievements, so she wrote in her history examination: "Abraham Lincoln was born on February 12, 1809, in a log cabin he built himself."

From a collection of boners made by English schoolchildren comes this one showing that the effect of American movies is very evident: A lad asked to identify the jungle figure Tarzan gave this definition: "Tarzan is a short name for the American flag. The full name is Tarzan Stripes."

Give it a chance and the humorous impulse lying dormant in some pupils will come out. Margaret Strom asked students to write a letter, as part of a ninth-grade English test, that some well-known person might have written during his life. Time was limited but one pupil's effort was magnificently brief and laughable. He wrote: "Dear Josephine, I am sorry to inform you that I did not make out so well at Waterloo. Yours truly, Napoleon."

The Double Blunder.

This particular type of humor arises from a compounding of errors which leads eventually to an embarrassing situation:

> At a college dance the young lady had just been introduced to her partner. By way of making conversation she commented as they waltzed around the ballroom floor, "Who is that terribly ugly man sitting over there?" Her partner looked at the man she indicated. "Why, that's my brother," he exclaimed. "Oh, you must excuse me," said the coed in embarrassment, adding apologetically, "I really hadn't noticed the resemblance."
>
> The guest at the faculty dinner party, arriving late, found a seat reserved for him near the head of the table, where a goose was being carved. "Oh," he exclaimed, "so I'm to sit by the goose." Then, observing the lady on his left, he made haste to amend an awkward phrase. "I mean," he said, "the roasted one, of course."

Absent-minded professors are in no way exempt from falling prey to the embarrassment of the two-time blunder. I daresay that most teachers too have at one time or another suffered through one:

> A very pretty Vassar girl, president of the school's science club, asked the biology professor to address the group. The professor rose: "I have worked closely with your president for a number of years," he said, "and during that time we have been intimate. . ." The group giggled and the professor tried valiantly to cover his slip: "And when I say intimate, I mean, of course, in a biological way."

Parent Perplexities.

It is more than a little incongruous that one of the hardest jobs of all—that of child rearing—is so often entrusted to amateurs. Sometimes parents wear out before the kids' shoes do.

The parent of one teen-ager says his hardest job is getting his son to realize that "no" can be a complete sentence. As everyone knows, some parents help their children with homework; others have children in accelerated programs. Automation may be with us but if you think everything these days is coin-operated, ask your teen-ager to shovel snow for a quarter. Fathers especially are perplexed to a point when it comes to their daughters.

> A traveler from California reports that a kid came home from school to ask his mother if she believed in "heterosexual premarital intradigitation." When she threatened to tell his father, he explained it means holding hands before marriage.
> *—Hugh Park, Atlanta Journal*

> A lady searched through the samples desperately in a dry goods store. "I simply have to find material with a metallic sheen and transparent enough to glow when a red bulb is lighted under it." The baffled clerk searched unsuccessfully. "No," he finally conceded, "we don't have it. But I'll order it if you tell me what on earth you need it for." "It's for my small son to wear in the school play," she replied exasperatedly. "Oh, if they only hadn't cast him as a nose cone!"

> Did you hear about the 13-year-old who played hooky from school, took $10 from the family's new car fund, went downtown, took in a movie, had a milkshake, played everything in the penny arcade and took a quarter chance on a new Dodge. His crime might still be undiscovered except that a man from the auto agency called on the boy's mother three days later and asked when her son wanted his new Dodge delivered.

My own daughters, now grown, once perceived happenings in ways that chiseled a chuckle in the patriarchal countenance.

> I was taking Dala, aged six, to school one frosty morning. As we backed out of the driveway and headed toward Westview School, the auto, as it often does on cold mornings, began to spit, sputter, shake and shudder. My patience short, I was obviously about to utter some caustic remarks under my breath when my companion of the morning admonished, "Now, daddy, take it easy. It's just shivering because it's cold."

Five-year-old Dlynn watched intently as the service station attendant filled the gas tank, checked the oil, and filled the battery with water, using a bulb syringe. As the last service was being performed, she looked up at me and asked, "Daddy, are they giving our car an enema?"

PTA Humor.

PTA meetings are notorious for "sameness"; that is, secretaries' reports, treasurer's reports, paper drives, projects A and projects B, etc. I have often thought of doing a one-man show, with me playing all the parts, depicting the stereotyped PTA meeting.

I scrapped the idea when it occurred to me that there is variety in PTA meetings. Strange things do happen. Some are funny.

A mother of nine children who was attending about her 500th PTA meeting jumped up and bolted from the room. "Goodness!" said one startled woman to another. "What got into her?" "Oh, nothing much," came the answer. "She suddenly realized she no longer had any kids in school."

Five little first graders marched out on the stage to welcome everyone at the PTA meeting. Each child carried a letter to make up the word "Hello." All took their correct positions except for one little boy who carried the letter "O." He couldn't remember where to stand. He paused for a few minutes at the back of the stage, much to everyone's amusement. But he really brought down the house when he finally decided he belonged at the head of the group.

The Fable.

In the first place the fable is fictitious. It may be a legendary story of supernatural happenings. Oftentimes animals play the role of people. The narratives which follow are examples of moralistic fables.

Once upon a time, according to an old fable, there were two frogs, one an optimist and the other a pessimist. It happened that the two frogs fell into a bucket of cream. The surface of the cream was so far below the brim that there was no way of getting out. At least, that is what the pessimistic frog decided. Convinced his situation was hopeless, he gave up and drowned. But the optimist frog looked at the side. He decided there had to be a way out, and that it would come to him sooner or later. Meanwhile, as he thought, he kept kicking his legs and swimming around and around. Before long the cream had turned to butter, and the frog who was an optimist jumped out.

An Aesop's Fable: Once upon a time there was a little red hen who scratched about and uncovered grains of wheat. She called her barnyard neighbors together and said, "If we work together and plant the wheat together we will have some fine bread together. Who will help me?" "Not I," said the pig. "Not I," said the goose, "Then I guess I will," said Red Hen, and she did. After the wheat started growing, the ground turned dry. "Who will help me water the wheat?" asked Red Hen. "Not I," said the goose. "Not I," said the pig. "Then I will," said Red Hen. The wheat grew tall into golden grain. "Who will help me reap the wheat?" asked Red Hen. "Out of my classification," said the pig. "I'll lose my aid to dependent children," said the goose. "I will," said Red Hen. She did. When it came time to grind the flour—"Not I," said the duck, "I'd lose my unemployment compensation." "Not I," said the cow. When it came time to bake the bread: "I'd lose my welfare benefits," said the pig. "If I'm the only one helping, that's discrimination," said the goose. "I'll do it myself," said the hen. She baked five loaves of fine bread. "I want some," said the duck. "I want some," demanded the goose." "Where is my share?" yelled the pig. "NO," said Red Hen. "I'll rest awhile, then eat them myself." "Excess profits," cried the duck. "Capitalistic leech," quacked the goose. "Company fink," grunted the pig. They hurriedly painted signs and marched around little Red Hen. The farmer came to investigate the noise. "You must not be greedy," he scolded little Red Hen. "But I planted the wheat. I watered it. I reaped it. I made the flour and baked the bread all by myself," said Red Hen. "Exactly," said the farmer. "That's the wonderful free enterprise system. Anybody in this barnyard can earn as much as he wants. You should be happy to have this freedom. In other barnyards you would have to give all five loaves to the farmer. Here you give four loaves to your long-suffering neighbors and get to keep one for yourself. You should be grateful." And so they all lived happily ever after, including the little red hen, who smiled and smiled, and clucked and clucked, "I am grateful, I am grateful." But her neighbors wondered why she never baked any more bread.

Satire.

Although it is unlikely that any storyteller ever won a jokeleaf cluster for spinning satire, some form of satire permeates—with the exception of fun with words and nonsense—most witticisms. Satire may be expressed in simple, pithy expressions or in longer essays.

> High school adviser to youth: "Your vocational-aptitude test indicates that your best opportunities lie in a field where your father holds an influential position."
>
> (*The Rotary Call*, Winnetka, Ill.)

> Locker-room conversation: "The coach's wife says he was deeply insulted by a mind reader; he was only charged half price!"

> Sign with new twist: "Watch out for school children—who are driving cars."

Plain Nonsense.

In this category we place all comic absurdities which don't fit too well elsewhere. They are foolish, without real meaning and contrary to common sense—yet there are those who say, "There's a lot of sense in nonsense."

There's a coloring book aimed particularly at educators. Herewith are some of the gems from *Coloring for Nerve Mastery* (Ego Publications, Westfield, Massachusetts):

> Here is my classroom. Count the desks. Can you count to 43?
> Here is my Principal. He collects Milk Money. He has a Master's Degree.
> Here is the milk for lunch. It is 10:15. Color the milk warm.
> This is our yellow School Bus. I like the yellow School Bus. It takes the children away.
> This is our Superintendent. I just flunked his son. Color the nice Superintendent purple.
> This is Report Card Day. This is my Telephone. Color the air Blue.

> Simple Simon met a pieman going to the fair. Said Simple Simon to the pieman, "Hello."
> Mary had a little lamb, its fleece was white as snow; and everywhere that Mary went, she took a bus.

Little Jack Horner sat in a corner, eating a Christmas pie; he put in his thumb, and pulled out a plum, and said, "Aw, nuts, I thought this was apple."

Hickory, dickory dock, the mouse ran up the clock; the clock struck one, the mouse ran down—I guess he couldn't take it.

Little Miss muffet sat on a tuffet, eating her curds and whey; there came a great spider that sat down beside her, and said,"Is this seat taken?"

Little Boy Blue, come blow your horn, the sheep's in the meadow, the cow's in the corn; but where is the boy that looks after the sheep? Oh, he's across the street having a soda.

Mistress Mary quite contrary, how does your garden grow? With cockleshells, and silver bells, and the rest haven't come up yet.

"Remember," said Professor Dimwit to his assembled class. "You cannot always be first. Take for example George Washington who was first in peace and first in war and first in the hearts of his countrymen. Well, he married a widow."

After the first two or three days of having the youngsters out of school, mothers begin to wonder why no one has gotten around to putting tranquilizers in chewing gum.

One of the biggest troubles with child psychology is that most children don't understand it well enough to explain it to their parents.

How, When and Where to Use Humor in Education

Humor is closely related to the emotion of joy about which Mark Twain wrote, "Grief can take care of itself, but to get the full value of joy, you must have somebody to divide it with." What better place than our schools to divide our joyful humor?

A sense of humor is a valuable quality and an asset in helping one to understand the incongruous. More than that, this sixth sense, humor, helps one to face his problems clearly. It makes living more enjoyable and adds zip and zest to human experience. Cultivating a sense of humor is not an automatic process, however, and exhortation is of little help.

We have reached a point in our relations with youth where it is simply pointless to continue playing the blame game. In this "erie era" of dealing with the "here and now" age we had better find more effective ways to relate, to motivate, to inspire. If education doesn't "make it," nothing makes it. Laughing together, enjoying together and sharing the low and high arcs of our psychic cycles all form one small but potent way to help education "make it."

Perhaps one essential of a happy and balanced life is a willingness to be amused. Therefore, says Ernst Renan, "Good humor is a philosophical state of mind; it seems to say to nature that we take her no more seriously than she takes us." Washington Irving wrote, "Honest good humor is the oil and wine of merry meeting, and there is no jovial companionship equal to that where the jokes are rather small and the laughter abundant."

According to Harry Overstreet, "Humor most deeply is a playful sense of those contrasts that we call incongruities. An

incongruity is something out of proportion and to be playfully
aware of the incongruity is the wisdom of humor." Thus, the
cognitive challenge. Humor is philosophy. As Will Durant
expressed it, "One is the essence of the other." Humor is
philosophy and philosophy is a love of wisdom. Alexander Pope
satirically pictured the stuffed scholar as follows:

> The bookful blockhead,
> Ignorantly read,
> With loads of learned lumber in his head.

Francis Bacon wrote, "Reading maketh a full man, but when
fullness means stuffiness, then fullness is insufficient." The humorous and playful man then can be just as intellectual as the
"bookful blockhead, ignorantly read." Perhaps humor can serve as
the liberty bell of the human mind. Again, the cognitive challenge!

Bishop Fulton J. Sheen once wrote that "Man is the only joker
in the deck of nature." He related the following legend: When
Adam was driven out of paradise, he complained bitterly before
his maker, "Where will I find comfort in my vast loneliness and
how will I obtain relief from my deep misery?" In response to his
plaintive cry, God presented Adam with a precious gift—a tear.
"This saline drop," said God, "is endowed with healing power. In
time of distress it will wash away your grief and relieve you of
your anxiety." Surely Adam received another gift—the ability to
laugh when things go wrong, for man is the only animal with the
ability to laugh and resort to humor when things go wrong.

I've noticed that most people become quite aroused if anyone
questions their sense of humor. They will go to great lengths to
prove that they do have that sixth sense. Really, it's hard to talk
about humor objectively—laughter, maybe, but not humor, for
there are multiple responses to humor.

On my visit to Russia I remember riding a city bus in Moscow,
walking in the streets, shopping and milling in hotel lobbies. There
was a dearth of mirth. Yet I know Muscovites have a sense of
humor, for it was most abundant at a Moscow circus I visited.
There was much joy and merriment—and teachers were a part of
it.

When he opened the 37th Congress of the International P.E.N.
Club in Seoul, President Change Hee Park of South Korea asked

members to use humor in an effort to ease world tension. Attended by 100 playwrights, authors and poets from 36 countries, the congress adopted the theme "Humor in the East and the West." Said Park, "Now more than at any other time, humor can play the role of tranquilizer to ease the tension and relieve the unrest of mankind in today's dehumanized society."

As far as therapy is concerned, the *Journal of the American Medical Association* came up with this one: "There isn't much fun in medicine but there's a great deal of medicine in fun." Think that one over and then plunge into the implications of Bill Mauldin's "Humor is really laughing off a hurt, grinning at misery." Teachers already know "hurt and misery." Isn't it reassuring to know that good humor is a relatively simple form of therapy?

Although there's much nonsense in humor, one also finds, if he looks, some sense in humor. Indeed, "The Sense in Humor" is the title of a provocative article in *Saturday Review* written by Harvey Mindess, a practicing psychologist and professor at UCLA. Wrote Professor Mindess: "The extent to which our sense of humor can help us to maintain our sanity is the extent to which it moves beyond jokes, beyond art, beyond laughter itself. It must constitute a frame of mind, a point of view, a deep-giving, far-reaching attitude to life." *You see, there is sense in humor. If psychologists and psychiatrists are finding it useful to encourage their patients' sense of the ridiculous as an antidote to emotional distress, surely we who teach can encourage our learners' sense of the ridiculous for an equally worthy end, that of preventing emotional distress.

Don't drag humor in by the heels; use it to make a point, relate it to the seasons, the holidays, and to current events. Who knows, you might even lay the keel for a future humorist or comedian. You could be proud of that.

If you're really interested "by the time you get to Phoenix" (that's the close of this section) you will find there some interesting and helpful sources of humor. Sure enough, some will require that you invest some money; others such as developing your own humor file and observing man cost little or nothing. Notice, I used the term "invest" for it is that. The few dollars you invest will return many hours of therapy in relief from tension and

---

*© by *Saturday Review World.* Used with permission.

anxiety and in the knowledge that you can help others to do the same.

> You're not too dignified for rumor
> And there's always time for humor.
> You cannot wait for a brighter hour,
> The time is now to use your humor power.

THE NATURE OF HUMOR*

What is humor? It is that soothing and compensating piece of the mind which prevents us from being overcome by life's adversities. Humor can dissipate the fog and make life more enjoyable and far less threatening. This is its chief function.

Much more should be said and written about humor for so many think it means no more than the ability to tell a funny story or to respond to one. Actually a sense of humor refers to a complete philosophy of life. It includes the ability to take it as well as to hand it out; it includes poise, the capacity to bend without breaking, taking life's responsibilities seriously but oneself not too seriously. A man who can laugh at himself will always be amused.

Other less obvious components of a sense of humor are these: the ability to relax, to escape from tension, to get pleasure out of the joys of others, to live unselfishly, laughing with people, not at them.

Humor is our sixth sense—as important as any of the other five. It creates happiness, fosters friendship, cheers the discouraged, and dissolves tensions. And, as a bonus, it frees the mind, oils the squeaks and enables us to carry on with fewer dark hours.

"Humor makes the educated mind a safer mind. The humorless intellectual is, of all personality cripples, one of the most handicapped and most disagreeable. He can be dangerous, too, as any force out of balance is dangerous. Though he prides himself upon his advanced mind and disdains the commonality, he is a poor exhibit of intellectualism . . . he lacks expression of spirit and, although he is always contentious, he is never the happy warrior."[1] When a man is both scholarly and funny he is usually a most effective communicator.

---

*For footnotes in this section, see REFERENCES on page 89.

A sense of humor is basically intellectual. It is, in part, a sense of proportion and ability to differentiate comparisons and contrasts. Incongruities are especially enjoyed . . . young people say they like teachers and leaders who have a sense of humor. But they want it to be good humor, too. They reject sarcasm.

It is not strange that the humor sense is so often found in great teachers and in youth leaders. It is surely a tonic to the teacher as well as to those he teaches. His ability to enjoy the incongruous serves him well. He may at times be a fool, but he will never, never be a pompous fool.

Nothing in man is more serious than his sense of humor; it is the sign that he wants all the truth, and sees more sides of it than can be soberly and systematically stated.[2] The world is a comedy to those that think, a tragedy to those that feel.[3]

In this era of science it is interesting to observe that today there are many scientists studying humor and there are many, many more scientists who are humorists. Perhaps a major task of science is to humanize itself through humor, a major humanizing instrument. In this way humor can be valuable in introducing an element of humility into the scientific approach.

Professor Robert Escarpit of the University of Bordeaux, widely known for his daily witty comment in the Paris newspaper *Le Monde,* points up the importance of humor for originality in scientific research. In his article, "Humorous Attitude and Scientific Inventivity," he remarks, "The scientist must not take himself seriously (the lunatic always does); only a sense of humor can guarantee that he remains intellectually open."

Psychologist Professor Harry F. Harlow, of the University of Wisconsin, points out that humor often has the objective of elevating one's own ego or social status. This is hardly surprising in view of his penetrating comment on the origin of humor: "Humor is born as we bare our teeth in laughter to ease the accumulating burdens we bear."

A sense of humor has affected the career of one scientist-professor James V. McConnel, University of Michigan, who reports negative repercussions because the scientific establishment takes science (with a capital S) to be sacred, something like religion. McConnel edits the Serio-Comic Scientific Journal called the *Worm Runner's Digest* [*worm runner*—trainer of worms]. He has conducted many studies on the common flatworm. McConnel reveals that he has been reprimanded for misleading students into thinking that science can be fun.

Because his *Worm Runner's Digest*, although seriously scientific, was permeated with humor, it was not taken seriously until there was a complete separation of the levity and the gravity. The humor is now at the back and printed upside down to prevent any possible confusion. His journal now has the title *The Journal of Biological Psychology*, to allow quotations to be made from it with suitable gravity.

McConnel sees his journal as the house organ of the anti-scientific (capital S) movement and laments that scientists are willing to make objective and dispassionate studies of any natural phenomena at will—except their own scientific behavior.

A similar light-hearted periodical, edited by Dr. Alexander Kohn of the Israel Institute for Bio Research and having 20,000 subscribers, is titled *The Journal of Irreproducible Results*. It is known as the journal in which scientists laugh at science. That's healthy! "Being a scientist," American Physicist Lee A. Dubridge has written, "does not disqualify a person from being an intelligent person." Nor, he might have added, from possessing a sense of humor.

Ample proof of both shows up in *A Stress Analysis of a Strapless Evening Gown and Other Essays for a Scientific Age*. Robert A. Baker, who has assembled this anthology of 32 articles and poems, says in his introduction that it's not unscientific to laugh, which is comforting in an age that put a man on the moon before it produced a garbage lid that fits.

Could it be that there is something in the moon's environment that causes joy and happiness? It does seem so, judging by the behavior of astronauts Conrad and Bean. They sounded exuberant as they went about their work during their first excursion into the hostile unknown.

The dangers they were exposed to were brought home when the television camera was knocked out by one brief, inadvertent exposure of the direct rays of the sun. But this did nothing to daunt the good spirits of Conrad and Bean. Instead, while this world listened, they continued to chatter, whistle, and sing as they went about the business of making man's second exploration of the moon.

There is, or at least seems to be, relatively little smiling, let alone audible expression of joy, in the workaday world. Even at play, adults, if not children, seem beset by a certain bitterness and seriousness. These are, to be sure, serious times. But the world could use some of the spirit of joy that Conrad and Bean displayed at work on the moon.

THE FUNCTIONS OF HUMOR

Drawing upon the wisdom of psychologists, philosophers and clowns, I have concluded that humor functions in a variety of ways:

1. as a social lubricant
2. as a safety valve
3. as therapy
4. as a tonic
5. as a sixth sense
6. as a survival kit
7. as motivation and cognitive challenge

Aware teachers and school leaders will surely recognize and perhaps capitalize upon one or more of these uses of humor in the educational enterprise.

Social Lubricant.

We are now in an age where it is imperative that people succeed to some extent in their social relationships. Such factors as more people in closer proximity, threats and instruments of violence as well as the threat of future shock, and more leisure, mandate easier, quieter, smoother relations among people of all sectors. This is just as true in our educational institutions as anywhere else.

No claim is made that humor alone is the one best social lubricant—but it can be a lubricant of some significance to human interaction in those trying hours between 8:30 and 3:30. That school world we look out on may be real, but even more important, I suggest, is the world we educators look out from. If we can look from a base of sunshine and humor rather than one of darkness and depression, there is greater hope that the moving parts in our social mix will be lubricated.

Safety Valve.

Psychoanalysts maintain that play is a way of mastering anxiety. Teaching the Pepsi generation makes teachers highly susceptible to anxiety, and since humor is a form of play, it is quite appropriate to think of the light approach as a way to master the malady. Learners, especially adolescents, also must handle the strains and stresses of their lives. For these reasons, humor in the school is helpful to the easing of aggressive impulses on the part of all persons involved.

Freud attributed pleasurable effects of humor stimuli to need gratification and tension reduction—therefore a tempering of anxiety. We must avoid the kind of humor which increases anxiety. It is difficult to justify scornful and sarcastic humor anywhere, let alone in the school. But it is well to remember this—it's no fun for a pupil to laugh at a teacher who can laugh at himself. The reverse applies. Therefore, we can conceive of humor as a safety valve against aggression, tyranny and persecution. We must laugh a little or a lot to keep from blowing our tops.

Therapy.

Without the ludicrous and ridiculous perception of objects and events one's journey through life would indeed be a bumpy one. Educators will always feel some bumps, most of which must be taken seriously—but not mournfully.

Man has access to a multiplicity of therapeutic aids to treat his psychological adversities. Good humor has a therapeutic effect on many mental ailments, say the psychiatrists. A laugh a day may keep the psychiatrist away.

We attribute the following philosophy to Romain Gary in "Promise at Dawn": "Humor is an affirmation of dignity, a declaration of man's superiority to all that befalls him." Teachers and administrators must not feel apprehensive about taking on the image of levity. Humorists are not clowns but most often men of great wisdom, as were the jesters and court fools in the medieval days.

Tonic.

It is rather generally agreed that our modern schools could

stand some regular injections of a tonic substance. Certainly they need no opiates. A tonic invigorates and stimulates the recipient. Properly applied, humor does that. It also restores and refreshes.

I know that humor works this way. I have ingested it as well as dispensed it with success. Naturally, some overly serious educators and some such pupils aren't ready for it. Our job is to make the tonic palatable. Someone has to make the move to create a school environment which is both thoughtful and joyful. Administrators and teachers have control. If they only had the inclination, the tonic effect of humor could be working now.

Sixth Sense.

More than once teachers have wished for more than the five senses they possess. And I'll bet that goes for some principals and a few students. Demands on everybody never seem to let up. Awareness and empathy in large measure are sorely needed in most of the interactions which occur in the name of education.

Art Linkletter said, "I've noticed that humor is a pretty good barometer of how a person is feeling, of his basic state of mind. It tends to go into eclipse when people are worried or unhappy or upset. If it disappears altogether, this may be a real danger signal. It may mean that the person's problems are getting stronger than he is.

So treasure your good humor, protect it and care for it. Keep it polished and available, not hidden away amid the anxieties and adversities of your mental closet. You just never know when you will want to call on your sense of humor, for so often it can compensate for lack of all the others."

Survival Kit.

Doubt is being expressed these days that the public school can survive. In some classrooms today somewhere some teachers wondered if they could survive the day. Since it all began, students have worried about completion of the semester, the year, or graduation requirements. Some school administrators today are known to celebrate each day of continued existence as a school leader. Everybody on the educational scene struggles, more or less, to survive. Some do; some don't . The load gets so heavy.

A knight in olden times, preparing to sally forth upon a long journey, thought it wise to provide himself against every emergency. For example, he put a mousetrap in his pocket lest he be troubled with mice. He hung a bee bonnet over his shoulder, lest he be pestered with bees. He put a mosquito net in his satchel lest he be annoyed by insects. And so on and so on. Finally he had such a load he could not carry it!

This is a parable of man's journey through life. We are prone to burden ourselves with so many elements of prevention that the load becomes impossible.

Will Shakespeare, who was no novice in humor matters, said it well, "A light heart lives long." All the players in the school game need the safety valve of humor to survive. When humor can be used as a defense against tribulations, it is truly functioning as a survival kit.

The survival ratio of those load-bearers who find it easy to laugh at themselves is relatively high. According to Jerry Lewis, black people and Jews are said to possess the greatest sense of humor simply because their safety valves have been working for centuries to make life bearable. If humor can do that much, perhaps it can cool down the classroom or the conference room.

Motivation and Cognitive Challenge.

Humor is philosophy. When one is a philosopher he is penetrating, comprehensive and flexible. So is the humorist. When it is not used as a weapon, humor is liberating, constructive and enabling. Even a joke may express a profound truth. Understanding some forms of humor, the joke for example, is an intellectual achievement. Therefore, it is cognitive, although it unavoidably elicits affective responses.

We are all aware of the games man plays. It is natural for man to apply his mental ability to puzzle and problem-solving. Humor is a puzzle until the responder understands it. Jacob Levine[4] said about motivation in humor, "Freud is the only theorist to regard humor as a fundamental psychological process that represents one of the two primary motivational bases for all behavior." Teachers would do well to keep in mind cognitive challenge as a factor in humor appreciation.

THE PHENOMENON OF LAUGHTER

What happened to laughter? America once was more of a laughing nation. Adults laughed and it was contagious. Children laughed as they played and socialized. Even the one-room little red schoolhouse rang with laughter. I know. I taught in one. Then we laughed easily and naturally.

Laughter and humor are not synonomous. For an analysis of laughter read *The Act of Creation* by Arthur Koestler. The spectators of old Rome laughed at the non-humor of Christians being tortured and killed.

Tests at Northwestern University Medical School show that laughter has a tonic effect on 95 percent of all people. Other tests at Fordham University bring out the fact that the act of laughing benefits more organs than a person thinks he has. When people laugh their diaphragms go up and down. This movement massages the right side of their hearts, causing the rate of their heartbeats to increase and providing a stimulating lift to their bodies.

Although humor and laughter are relatively unexplored by scientists, even these aspects of human behavior have their experts. For laughter the man is Dr. William A. Fry of Stanford University. He admits that medical literature in no way indicts laughing, yet—somewhat contrary to the Fordham University conclusions—he thinks that one can laugh too much, causing hernias, duodenal ulcers, and possibly strokes for the susceptible subjects.

Ulcers, someone once said, come as a result of mountain climbing over molehills. In the midst of the Civil War Abe Lincoln once remarked, "If I did not laugh, I think I should die."

In the *Indiana Freemason,* Sir Max Beerbohm wrote, "Strange when you come to think of it, that of all countless folk who have lived on this planet, not one is known in history or in legend as having died of laughter."

According to Ecclesiastes, there is a season for everything: "A time to weep and a time to laugh." "A laugh is worth a hundred groans in any market," said Charles Lamb; and Victor Hugo declared that he likes laughter that opens the lips and the heart. Serious-minded Carlyle avowed, "How much lies in laughter—the cipher key, wherewith we decipher the whole man!" According to

Herbert Spenser, laughter is the indication of an effort which suddenly encounters a void. Or in Kant's expression, "Laughter is the result of an expectation which suddenly ends in nothing." Allin's theory is that laughter arises because of cerebral congestion or torpidity of blood circulation. According to Bergson, laughing is a human phenomenon—only humans laugh—humor is human! A number of psychologists agree that the effect of laughter is, in most cases, to relieve tension or congestion of some sort in the body and the mind. This is known as the relaxation theory of laughter. There are various versions of the relaxation theory: one theory is that laughter is due to subconscious satisfaction, Freud proposes the theory of economy of psychic expenditure and relief from inhibitory and repressive processes, and Crile says laughter is the result of psychological clarification. McDougall has expressed the opinion that human beings have evolved laughter as an antidote to suffering and pain. Essentially he said, "To laugh is to temper pain if not altogether to remove it." [5] How about that? Ecclesiastes, Lamb, Hugo, Carlyle, Spenser, Kant, Bergson, Freud. That should satisfy your intellectual hunger.

Where have all the clowns gone? There is so much to laugh about, yet the 20th century has not produced a Mark Twain or a Will Rogers. Humor magazines and humorous columnists are noticeably lacking. After-dinner speeches for the most part only add to the listeners' need to consume anti-gas pills. This is a ripe subject for a lively argument, particularly among those who prefer to laugh at the foibles of frailty. After all, we are very funny, aren't we?

One of man's greatest salvations is that the spirit of comedy and laughter often works where all else fails. It may function either as a shield or as a weapon. According to Freddie Trenkler, the Ice Capades clown, laughter is the greatest thing in the world. Said Trenkler, "I love to hear the sound of laughter. That's what keeps me young. It's music, pure music." I wonder, I wonder how many teachers love to hear the sound of children and teen-agers laughing! I do know that youngsters love to hear adults laugh. Yet according to George Condon in the *Cleveland Plain Dealer,* "There is nothing quite so difficult for a man to do as laugh, and yet there is nothing that produces such satisfactory results. Laughter is the most devastating deterrent to pomposity, ego and all the other sickening forms of self-satisfaction."

"Actually animals cannot smile and do not laugh," says Grotjahn.[6] Through their bodies rather than through symbols, they express emotions. Laughter communicates but is less sophisticated than speech. Body language expresses laughter. This primitive aspect of behavior was well known to Lord Chesterfield, who admonished his son that a gentleman was never caught laughing aloud. Forget Lord Chesterfield's advice.

Laughter has more than once saved the day, the hour, the minute. As we have previously indicated, laughter is primarily social and, to a limited extent, a form of language. Since laughter is one of our freedoms, let's not lose it. It is the cheapest luxury man enjoys. As T. Harry Thompson put it, "It stirs up the blood . . . expands the chest . . . electrifies the nerves . . . cleans away the cobwebs from the brain and gives the whole system a cleansing rehabilitation."

The desire to laugh is a basic human craving. Enormous amounts of money and effort are expended in radio, TV and theater to promote laughter. Research on laughter, however, is very limited. A notable exception is the work of Jacob Levine who has been making studies of humor for 25 years. Some of his research, reported in the *Scientific American*, reveals some provocative dimensions of laughter.

It takes real genius these days to make people laugh. The gift of laughter-making is one of the rarest and most precious things God gave to man. The Lord loves a laughin' man. Attributed to the late John F. Kennedy is this bit of wisdom: "There are three things in life which are real . . . God, folly and human laughter . . . Since we don't do much about the first two, we must do what we can about the third."

Rabelais spoke, "One inch of joy surmounts of grief a span because to laugh is proper to the man." Lesser-known Bob Moekler, as quoted by Goddard in the St. Louis *Globe Democrat,* spoke, "Laughter is like a diaper change. It doesn't solve any problems permanently . . . just makes life a bit more comfortable for a while."

In human relationships laughter often serves as a green light, a light in the darkness and a prop for our "leaning" time. Man is the risible animal and the social primacy of laughter is certainly a significant factor in his capacity to surface again and again after life's burdens have caused him to submerge.

Thanks to Jack Crawford for this light verse:

> When a bit of sunshine hits ye, after passing of a cloud,
> When a bit of laughter gits ye, and ye'r spine is feelin' proud,
> Don't forget to up and fling it at a soul
> That's feelin' blue,
> For the minute that ye sling it
> It's a boomerang to you.

Next time you feel like Jello looks when it is set in movement, when you have the jitters, try a good laugh. The ability to get a good laugh out of everyday situations is a safety valve for many of your enervating afflictions.

Believe it or not, there is a National Laugh Foundation with a powerful federation of laughmakers. January of 1966 marked the beginning of a Humor Lobbyist in Washington. The purpose of this registered funny man was to bring humor into politics, constructively, and to help lawmakers use humor as a tool for the public welfare. In this book, I like to think I am lobbying to bring humor into education so that it is used by all concerned as a means for uplifting all concerned.

HUMOR AND THE CHILD

Where does education begin? Surely it begins in play and continues in play for all our lives. Yet no sooner does education become formalized than it becomes solemnized. The current debate over education is largely between two solemnities: education for adjustment to life versus education for the development of the mind. Behind both is the pragmatic premise that education, like play, is worthless in itself. The purpose of play is to develop the spirit of cooperation or the sense of sportsmanship or the strength of mind and body (so that they may be employed in important tasks). But formal education is still a solemn enterprise.

Although the relation between intellectual prowess and response to humor stimuli is not clearly known, it is obvious that a measure of cognition is needed to understand the intellectual demands posed by certain forms of humor. Zigler, et al.[4] reviewed the literature on the relation of intellect and humor response and also conducted some appropriate research. They demonstrated with children in grades two through four that as children grew to understand a group of 25 cartoons their mirth responses also increased. Similar results for fifth graders were expected but didn't materialize. With these youngsters mirth scores decreased. It was concluded that mere comprehension of a humor piece does not guarantee a response of mirth. A mirth response is a response of glee and gaiety, typically accompanied by laughter.

It was conjectured that the cartoon contents offered no cognitive challenge for the older children. Such evidence suggests that perhaps only cartoons which are neither too demanding nor too easy elicit the humor response. The variable and key factor therefore must be the appropriateness of the intellectual demand posed by the humor. Essentially this means that congruence of humor stimulus complexity and the child's cognitive complexity produces the greatest mirth response.

Grotjohn[6] concluded that "a sense of humor signifies emotional maturity." His theory holds that the humor sense as a trait blooms after the child has grown to understand jokes and comic utterances or experiences. After he has matured somewhat in his social relationships and in self-acceptance then he is more likely to acquire a sense of humor, a cherished trait which serves to integrate his self-acceptance and tolerance of others.

Fry[7] found that the riddle was attractive to children in the age range of five to eight. Though riddles are rarely of much interest to adults, it appears that they represent for children suitable experiences for formalizing cognitive behavior.

Anecdotal humor appeals to children just a little older. The six-year-old may not be amused by the anecdote while the eight-year-old shows a keen interest in anecdotal humor involving adults. The transition is often imperceptible. Here is another bit of evidence pointing to comprehension as the determiner of response or no response. The affective impact, however, may also be a factor. At any rate the mirth response indicates the capacity to grapple with the intellectual aspect of the humor presented.

Teachers are reminded that most normal children enjoy using their thought power to solve puzzles or problems, to invent things and untangle mysteries. "Getting" the point in humor pieces is a similar mental exercise. According to Fry, slapstick is most appreciated by pre- and early-adolescents. Some abstraction is required to interpret it along with some insight into interpersonal behavior. Instruction-minded teachers are prone to regard as unscholarly that category of humor known as slapstick. Fry reminds skeptics that slapstick was part of the way of life and entertainment in ancient Egypt and Greece.

It is true, as Alfred North Whitehead said in his study of the *Aims of Education,* that: "For successful education, there must always be a certain freshness in the knowledge dealt with. It must either be new in itself or it must be invested with some novelty of application to the new world of new times. Knowledge does not keep any better than fish. You may be dealing with knowledge of the old species, with some old truth; but somehow or other it must come to the students, as it were, just drawn out of the sea and with the freshness of its immediate importance." Humor is freshness.

Humor is a vital part of our culture. It gives us a sense of perspective in a life cluttered with trivia and tragedy. Humor is also a major form of education; much of our knowledge of Shakespeare comes more through parodies and jokes than through a study of the men themselves.

Studies in psychology have explored the hollows of laughter, and some findings confirm what you may have long suspected. "We laugh more when we have been under tension than when we are relaxed. Men find more humor in stories of hostility and aggression than do women, and women laugh more at nonsense than do men. (Is this why women laugh at men?) One study of children's humor shows that the kids find adults to be very funny; the moron stories are not about a little moron but about an adult moron."[8]

Laughter is no joke to Dr. William Fry, Jr. Fry has devoted 18 years of research to chortles, giggles and guffaws, learning among other things that they disrupt breathing, increase the heart rate and interfere with brain waves. But laughter also helps humans handle their frustrations and fears. Fry, a psychiatrist who is in private practice and also on the clinical staff of Stanford University School of Medicine, believes humor is "one of our major coping mechanisms." He said: "It helps us cope with things distressful and challenging, with potential violence, and with reconciling new elements in our thinking. That's why most people who teach or lecture use humor as a vehicle for education." It also plays a stimulating role in life "because it is the essence of humor to be creative—in the sense of its revealing hidden and unexpected relationships."[8]

The other day I got to wondering why there aren't some amateur comedians available to add a laugh or two at meetings of local clubs, and entertain at hospitals or nursing homes. There are amateur singers, violinists, pianists, tap dancers and speakers. But few amateur comedians or humorists, the kind of entertainers most audiences would really enjoy, seem to exist.

"Many people are convinced that children have to be born with an appetite for wit; otherwise they are fated to live out their lives as gloomy Guses and mournful Maudes. It isn't so. When youngsters are exposed to humor, they have a good chance of acquiring a taste for it."[9] Home and school expose children to literature, music, and other of life's good things. "Why not include a portion of fun in the diet?" asks Sam Levenson.

Does a youngster really need a sense of humor? You might as well ask if he needs to be vaccinated against smallpox. I have found that there is nothing in prescriptions or on the couch that can match the stuff that makes people laugh.

A sense of humor may help a youngster at school. A University of Florida professor found through a series of tests that those students who showed the greatest ability to appreciate humor got the best grades. His humorless students usually got low grades. When facing problems of learning, remember that humor is an important balance wheel.

What laughter is, and why it is, and what is a sense of humor and how you get it, what a joke is, and why it is a joke—all these things remain unknown and unascertained. In a world that studies and teaches everything that can be studied and taught, humor alone remains as an unexplored field.

Few people know anything about humor, or analyze or think about it. It is left completely out of the program of self improvement. A man will work hard on such things as his game of golf. It is pathetic to see a stout man trying hard to improve his mashie shot, a thing which God forbade to him at birth. But still he tries, yet would he ever seek to improve his sense of humor, ever practice his funny story, or ever read a book on how to tell one? For all other literary and artistic requirements there are classes and courses, schools and colleges. People with a talent for music take music lessons. Children with a gift for drawing are taught art. But no one teaches funny boys humor.[10] Teaching humor would not mean teaching people to make fun of things, but teaching people to understand things. Humor, at its highest, is a part of the interpretation of life.

Laughter and good humor are as contagious as depression and dourness. School children respond, inevitably, to the teacher's disposition. These illustrations are poignant:

> I was good at everything.
> —Honest, everything!
> Until I started being here with you.
> I was good at laughing,
> Playing dead,
> Being kind!
> Yeah, I was good at everything!
> But now I'm only good at everything
> On Saturdays and Sundays.
>
> When you don't like me, teacher,
> I feel the whole world sees me in wrinkled pants.
> Or in my underwear or no pants on.
> I know I'm not very smart.
> And sometimes I laugh when I shouldn't
> But I don't want to go home with you not liking me.
> Please!
> Choose me to wash the blackboards at three o' clock!
>
> Teacher, let me swim in a puddle,
> Let me race a cloud in the sky,
> Let me build a house without walls.
> But most of all,
> Let me laugh at nothing things.
>
> I couldn't help it!
> I tried to hold it back! I tried hard!
> I couldn't help it that I pooped!
> Everyone giggled except you.
> You gave me a dirty look.
> Why didn't you smile if you've forgotten how to laugh?
> At least until the redness went out of my face.[11]

"There is a strange unhappy philosophy afoot whose adherents insist that education must never be fun—that laughter and learning are incompatible. I feel assured that these prophets of gloom have always been on the scene, though. No doubt the sound of laughter emanating from Plato's academy raised many a Greek eyebrow.

Shakespeare recognized the need for comic relief, even in the presence of death, but the pallbearer school of pedagogues steadfastly declines to accept the truth about people—that, where there is no joy, there is no real life or growth."[1][2]

In recent months several publications have reached my desk which indicate probably a slight turn in the direction of more personality, dynamism, verve, color, humor and feeling on the part of the teacher. Among these publications were such titles as "Teaching with Feeling," "How You Can Become an Exciting Teacher" (a record album), "Schools Without Failure," "Teaching Power," and "The Human Side of Teaching." Each in its own way makes the point that enthusiasm, kindness, warmth and feeling are contagious at least to an equal degree with apathy, aloofness and drabness. In her own way Mother Goose gave us a vivid pic of the situation: "Cross Patch! Draw the latch. Sit by the fire and spin, take a cup, drink it up, (kindness), then call your neighbors in."

Does school have to be fun? Maybe not, but it helps. Most children enter school with great expectations. They are intrigued by what lies ahead though they are not at all sure what it's going to be. Along the way they encounter, if they are lucky, teachers who make learning an adventure. A teacher can interest students in how they make rope in Pago Pago if she is dramatic and enthusiastic.

In education, how and why do we ever stray away from some requirements we know must exist in the exciting teacher? Flair, humor, lesson dramatization and a ready smile can and do prevent boredom. If we had our way, every teacher would be required to have training and experiences in simple dramatics. Since this is not likely to happen soon, let's concentrate on the last of the above qualities, a ready smile.

A car rental corporation has done a pretty thorough job of putting before America's traveling men a smiling face. Now it has embarked on a new campaign with the captivating slogan, "Behind every smile a brain," which is the company's way of emphasizing its objective of serving the public through personnel who are both pleasant and efficient. Great care has been taken to train and prepare girls to handle their duties effectively and to meet emergencies skillfully. I propose a new campaign to improve teaching. The slogan is "In front of every brain a smile." It is probably true that teachers of this era generally are better prepared academically and are intellectually more capable of handling "brain" tasks than the teachers of bygone days. But there is simply no evidence that they can or do smile more than their earlier counterparts. And there must be some truth in the saying "One smile just might warm three cold winter months." If it means so much to so many youngsters, why are we in teacher education not more concerned with the countenance?

How to smile: enlarge the oral orifice both horizontally and vertically in such a way that its corners turn up sufficiently to reveal the incisors. Inevitably this at least to some extent wrinkles the skin surrounding the lateral areas of the eyes. For a full effort the eyes must reflect an inner glow. A smile is born! We need one in front of every brain.[1 3]

Uses of humor in school are multiple: (1) as a tension reducer, (2) to make a point, (3) as a preoccupation breaker, (4) a humor convocation, (5) to develop amateur humorists—why not? We teach sewing, serving, welding, cake baking, driving, etc. What happens when a pupil exhibits his humor, becomes funny in school? He's sent to the principal or the counselor. Why not teach humor and teach with humor?

One teacher describes another: "Jim teaches much the way classical story tellers teach. He tells a story or a joke or an anecdote you might understand. He gives you something of his own experience and maybe you can learn something from it if you are ready. And because he is such a fine story teller he listens too because he is learning all the time, expanding his repertoire, trying to come to terms with experience without destroying it."[1 4]

The ability to make others laugh is a rare and precious commodity. Those blessed with this gift should not hide or repress it but should cultivate this talent and share its delights with local groups.

LAUGHTER AND LEARNING

Learning begins in pleasure and thrives in curiosity. To be specific, young learners ought to laugh greatly, for laughter is a high priority principle for learning. It signifies a general self-sacrifice to mutuality. General laughter offers security and since it is pleasurable, it is a motivator. Since it has a liberating effect, it buoys the spirit of discovery.

Our current emphasis on humanizing education is well justified. Grotjahn agrees. "Everything done with laughter helps us to be human. Laughter is a way of human communication which is essentially and exclusively human. It can be used to express an unending variety of emotions. It is based on guilt-free release of aggression, and any release makes us perhaps a little better and more capable of understanding one another, ourselves, and life. What is learned with laughter is learned well. Laughter gives freedom, and freedom gives laughter. He who understands the comic begins to understand humanity and the struggle for freedom and happiness."[6]

Theodore M. Hesburgh, President of the University of Notre Dame, has written: "Two qualities—laughter and love—are vital to bridging the generation gap ... too many of the young have forgotten how to laugh, and too many of their elders have forgotten how to love." This is a provocative linking of two emotions and an indictment to both sides of the gap if indeed one exists. I suspect that Hesburgh has given an accurate observation.

If laughter relieves tensions it also warms the heart, minimizes unnecessary concern and enables one to perceive reality more clearly. All this is bound to have a profound and positive effect on learners. In addition the teacher also benefits in yet another way, for laughter is an aid to beauty at any age.

Complaining, inveighing, lamenting, criticizing, sleeping, eating, working and frittering consume most of our time. In his book, *Applied Imagination,* Alex Osborn told of the Swiss gentleman of eighty who concluded mournfully, "I figure that I have laughed for only 46 hours in my entire life."

Research evidence and observation suggest that the spontaneous laugher is likely to own a healthy perspective on life. Easy laughers tend to be more sensitive and sympathetic than those whose countenances are offered to the world unsmiling and joyless. An old French proverb offers this profound wisdom: "The day is lost in which one has not laughed."

Laughing and playing need not be beneath teachers. We can be exuberant without being foolish. To maintain this free world requires that we make fun of it. It's a freedom we cannot afford to lose. More laughter in our schools might do as much as anything else to combat the stormy anger in our rabble rousers.

Let a smile be your umbrella, teachers. "Use humor," advises psychologist George Cheviakov, "by encouraging the class to laugh together. The mere physical process of laughing automatically neutralizes anger."[15] Laughter is infectious.

Even pompous teachers and administrators are very funny because they believe that their pomposity somehow obscures their intellectual insecurity. To be noticed they must keep the act going. Thomas Hobbes suggested, "The passion of laughter is nothing but sudden glory arising in ourselves from sudden conception of some eminency in ourselves by comparison with the inferiority of others or with our own—formerly."

LAUGHING AT ONE'S SELF

To become accomplished in the engaging art of laughing at yourself, you must be able to see yourself through the eyes of others and laugh at what registers on the retina. Think of the power in that teacher's hands who invites his pupils to laugh with him at his mistakes. His pupils feel no threat whatsoever in his self-directed humor. Why is that teacher who "puts himself down" so amusing? Partly because there's a touch of despair in us all and it's comforting to children, and to youth particularly, to hear the teacher laugh at his own discomfiture.

The folly of taking one's self too seriously is nowhere more evident than in education. When we laugh at ourselves, we have a healthy perspective and are able to neutralize our shortcomings. That teacher who can relate a riotous description of his own "goofs" is not likely to have to hear others do it.

Charles Schulz, the father of Charlie Brown, wrote, "If I were given the opportunity to present a gift to the next generation it would be the ability for each individual to learn to laugh at himself." More teachers ought to feel like Schulz. "Know thyself" is a much less dangerous maxim when it is supplemented by "Laugh at thyself."

When it is used thoughtfully, laughter is sunshine in the

schoolhouse. We laugh best when others laugh with us. Children's laughter, when directed with ours, lets the best that is in us all shine out. The highest and the finest laughter of all is the laughter of the man, especially the man of high position, who laughs at himself.

One way for teachers to meet the challenge of instructional problems is to learn the art of laughter. Most of all, learn to laugh at yourself. "He who laughs, lasts!"[16] A teacher who can laugh at himself will always be amused.

JOY IN THE SCHOOLS

When the Indians were running this country, there were no taxes, no national debt, and the women did all the work. The white man thought he could improve on a situation like that! When Running Bear saw his first lighthouse, he stood there, arms folded tightly, and said, "White man blow'em horn, white man blink'em light, but the fog rolls in."

In nearly all of its aspects modern living is a foggy experience. Education has not escaped and clear days in education have recently been fewer in number. Student activism is a blessing. Student activism is a blight. Each side has its supporters. Teacher assertiveness is a virtue to a point. To what point? As educators we point with pride and view with alarm. The fog is in, and as Dickens suggested in his *Tale of Two Cities*, "It is the best of times, it is the worst of times."

In our nation's schools, particularly our secondary schools, there is a high priority issue which has received far too little attention. It is not race relations, it is not ecology, and it is not drugs. It is not discipline. Above all it is not fashionable. To my knowledge it has not been the theme of any workshop; no paperbacks in the book stores deal with it. No demonstrations of any importance have occurred on its behalf; and yet it is crucial, cutting across all class and ethnic lines. It is a gut issue for the vast majority of youth and their parents.

American secondary education which is much to my taste in most matters has one frightful weakness. It has not devised any sensible way of promoting joy in its institutions of learning, nor does it now show capabilities for solving the problem. Perhaps it is too great a task to make joyful that period of time youngsters spend in our schools. The idealism expressed in the words of one song, " . . . teach the world to sing in perfect harmony, with apple trees, honey bees and snow white turtle doves," may be beyond our reach.

It doesn't hurt now and then to look back and count our wins and our losses. If we are honest and discerning we can measure both victories and defeats as well as identify the challenges that lie ahead. Where did we succeed? Where did we fail? We succeeded where we cared enough to accept and respect the learner and his culture. We succeeded where we reached understanding of and respect for the parents' situation. We succeeded where we were perceptive enough to involve parents both in the learning and in the teaching. We succeeded where we performed effectively our enabling role as educators. We succeeded where we recognized the worth and potential of the individual, where we communicated our high though reasonable expectations for youth and their parents. We succeeded where we made possible that stab of joy for many learners. Where did we fail? We failed where our caring was superficial and discriminatory. We failed where our rigid routines and organizational structure stood in the way of human inter-action and when we dehumanized people. We failed when we underestimated human potential in minority people and in social classes lower than middle. We failed where joy was not abundant.

What is joy? General semantics tells us that words don't have meaning. Only people do. It is likely therefore that in your minds there are scores of different meanings for this word, *joy*. I can guess that some of them are delight, gaiety, happiness, pleasure, well-being, exuberance, good fortune, success, achievement, and just plain fun. I see the implications of all of these but to me joy also suggests an inner harmony with one's physical and human environment. Pupils, teachers, principals all are constantly reach-ing for that inner harmony.

To perform a task or role better than most and to reap the recognition for having done it contribute to the full and useful life. A succession of failures in school, with not even a smell of success, is chiefly responsible for the negative self-image which in turn is a major cause of delinquency. Schools that do not have any failure may be an impossibility; schools built on the promise of considerable success are both vital and possible.

Sometime or other we must face the fact that everybody is a somebody. Each somebody wants, needs and should have one or more peak experiences in junior and senior high school. It is disappointing to learn that so many undergraduates arrive on our campus without a history of peak experiences, recognition, spotlight, limelight, or whatever you choose to call it; at best their self-image is neutral. Education must be so designed as to ensure one or more peak experiences for each boy and girl. Only then can the American dream for education become real, and we can turn the wrecker into a builder, the spectator into a performer, and the delinquent into a citizen.

We live in a society that guarantees many wants and needs. The Bill of Rights guarantees us freedom of speech and the right to trial by jury. When we are dissatisfied with a product, we take it back to the store and get a refund or replacement. And with the replacement we may get a guarantee of 90 days, one year, or even five years. In other words, we guarantee nearly everything in our society—except joy and success in school. Not only do we not guarantee success and joy in school, we tend to deny them in the very procedures we use to promote their growth and to evaluate the results.

Although some analytic observers disagree, articles in various publications these days announce that the youth revolution—or the youth movement—is over. Whatever it was it made such an impact that our society is more than ever influenced by our young. American people of all ages are now faced with the necessity of recognizing and living with the profound changes youth has wrought in the past few years.[17]

The movement may or may not be over, but the idealism and altruism of youth are enduring facts. As Maria Montessori observed, "A corn seed knows how to become a corn stalk as it grows. If rain is lacking, a seed may not properly fulfill its destiny. But it will continue to try, to the end."

Adult society has made it possible for youth to become aware of such late 20th century phenomena as the population explosion, the knowledge explosion and the technology explosion. Perhaps one explosion which has not been brought dramatically to the attention of our young people by teachers, parents and other youth leaders is the opportunity explosion.

In this creative, everchanging, "daily-idea" society of ours, opportunity has never been so generous; yet the young are somewhat myopic or somehow unwilling to recognize it. Some of them never see an opportunity because it so often masquerades as a hard job, an undignified role, or a "kickless" monotony. Others sense the existence of opportunities but foolishly seize only a small measure. Can you imagine anyone looking at the rushing, tumbling, sparkling waters of opportunity and saying,"I'll take a cupful," or even the more unaware soul who, in an uncertain voice, entreats, "Just a thimbleful for me." Still others play with opportunities as children do at the seashore. They fill their hands with sand and then let the grains sift through, until all are gone.

Already it's too late for those youth of the herd who upon reaching their first destination crisis chose the "up, up and away" route on the wings of drugs to nowhere. Little did they know then that four things come not back—the spoken word, the sped arrow, the past life and the neglected opportunity. To those youth and their parents who care enough to ask where the best opportunities for the future lie, we in education must answer quickly, "They exist within people themselves."

We must do even more. Dramatically and convincingly we must communicate the idea that an opportunity is found in every obligation. In a very real sense obligating oneself to live and work responsibly is one giant step toward maturity. To those maturing youth who seek obligations and assume responsibilities the opportunity explosion will become a joyful reality.[18]

Although I am not quite sure what it means to them, young people are quite willing to express a desire for joy. I strongly suspect that acceptance, approval, liberation from unnecessary restraints, a joyful and harmonious home, an adequate self-concept, something useful to do, a progressive community, some success and a peaceful world would add up to joy and happiness.

The fact that the young have strong feelings about eradicating human despair, misery and suffering, futile conflict, and intolerance of differences in others is a positive if not always a realistic approach. After all, there is something of the genius in those who pick targets others cannot see and hit them. Let us not put them down for wanting happiness.

Were each of us to acquire an appreciation for joy in the educational enterprise in his respective orbit, we would soon appreciate the role of exuberance in society, for it may be the only mood and spirit that can provide freedom from monotony and discouragement. Try it.

Perhaps the first instructional task of today's principal is to determine through a teacher's everyday tasks whether she truly cares about her pupils and their happiness. The first essential of a happy life is a willingness to be amused. Most children are willing. How about teachers and principals?

What we need in our time is a mature realism which makes us understand that the human predicament is with us to stay. We shall not eliminate sin in others and we shall not eliminate it in ourselves. We shall not achieve utopia in our schools, though we can make some things relatively better than they are. Meanwhile we are wise to learn again to laugh, primarily at ourselves.

No matter whether you're carrying crowns or crosses, it's good therapy and good behavior to be both the architect and the consumer of humor and joy in our schools.

1. Everybody needs to feel like somebody. Ask any psychiatrist. More people need their heads swelled than shrunk.
2. Try guaranteeing some success and joy.
3. Where there is not joy, there is no real life or growth.
4. Good humor is an expression of joy, and vice-versa.
5. Humor is a part of the interpretation of life.
6. A laugh a day keeps the psychiatrist away.
7. A man who laughs at himself will always be amused.
8. Unstring your bows now and then.
9. Be the happy warrior.

SOURCES OF HUMOR

Educators work hard at lesson planning, paper grading and getting ready for the negotiations table. They lie awake at night trying to come up with workable ways to prevent and treat misbehaving youth. They read and go to classes, workshops and conferences to learn the ways of motivation. Rarely do they purposefully plan to improve their humor quotient, something which could smooth many rough spots for themselves and their learners.

The humor parade in schools is at best haphazard, and educationally the humor of our times is in need of some rejuvenation. Where does a humor-minded teacher start? Where can one see, enjoy and take unto himself humor sufficient to help him become a transmitter, consumer and mediator of the levity of life?

Humor is everywhere, though the seeker must hone his powers of observation and perception. Analysis of one's own behavior eventually reveals some self-deflating humor, the kind that keeps us humble and in balance with man and nature. A teacher can be his own source of amusement but first he must sense it and admit it.

The family unit offers a broader base for observing and enjoying humor. The family that laughs together stays together. Acquiring an awareness of the presence of fun happenings in the family is a first priority. With self and family as a starting point, a teacher next becomes aware of the humorous in his ever growing circle of friends, social groups, clubs and recreational activities. He can become to greater or lesser degrees the consumer, the reporter and even the producer of that tonic which makes adversity and disappointment more manageable—humor.

Obviously the school itself is a rich source of humor. Most kids are bent on fun, although their humorous expressions and antics are little appreciated, much less capitalized upon for the teacher's present and later use as elements of richer living and teaching.

It may be surmised that a low percentage of teachers make any organized effort to capture the words of wit, the boners, the gags and all the other forms of humor uttered by their learners. Yet every time I have discussed this matter with teachers, they usually recall with glee at least one such "funny." Why shouldn't a teacher include a humor file along with all the myriad others? No reason at all other than apathy. Forget apathy! Start the humor file. In no more than ten years a humor-minded teacher can have enough examples in the bank to draw interest for time to come and at the same time be well on the way to becoming an expert in "schumor." That word "schumor" is of my own coinage, a happy wedding of school and humor. It may never make Webster, but it just made this book.

But humor is to be found everywhere as I said earlier, not just in the self, the home, one's social experiences and at school, but literally everywhere. Wherever you are and whatever you do, observe carefully, and report what you see, and above all think humor. Chances are great that in the observation or the reporting, and perhaps in both, humor will rise.

Naturally, there are other sources of humor which might be classified as secondary sources. In other words something other than original personal perceptions and reactions may be involved. I have found that radio and television commercials, announcements and pronouncements can be both actual and potential sources of humor. Of course, the imagination must be in high gear. Here are to be found slips of the tongue, wordplays and subtleties which amuse the amusable mind. A television talk show host was recalling an interview with an entertainment star. He casually remarked, "Deep down, she's really very shallow."

Mere examination of newspapers, bulletins, newsletters, magazines reveals occasional slips in type, misplaced modifiers and other such unintended errors. This statement was spotted on the editorial page of an educational journal: "Points of view expressed in this quarterly are not necessarily condoned or even understood by the editorial staff." One school paper carried the following news item: "At the school Home Economics carnival last Saturday, Sally Walker won the pie baking contest. Her pie was judged to be most satisfying to the taste bads." The classified ad section of newspapers and magazines is a rather well-known garden of gems for the humor hunter: "New apartments for rent. Holly Hill deluxe units, near school, children welcome, also furnished." These are both intended and unintended, I suspect.

To this point attention has been called to the kinds of humor created by human imperfections. Maybe we can call them the "foibles of frailty"! Telling a bedtime story to his son, a labor leader began, "Once upon a time and a half. . . ." The more affected one gets with humor hunger the more he learns of the sources of what it takes to satiate him. The point is simply that the hunter's hunting grounds begin to enlarge. Let's start with buying, borrowing or at least reading funny books. They are humorous not by accident but by design, as are the sources which follow in this book.

Fortunately, there are some, though not enough, humorous books to please the fancy of the teachers' lighter side. We are likely to think of Twain's books and although they are funny and worth reading and re-reading, they are dated as far as humor is concerned. Dick Gregory's *From the Back of the Bus* supports my thesis that there is humor in the truth of things. His book is both funny and true. "Clever," "witty," and "delightfully funny" are the best words I know to describe a little paperback titled, *Just Wait Till You Have Children of Your Own.* The authors are Erma Bombeck and Bill Keane and the publisher is Fawcett Publications, Greenwich, Conneticut.

Other humorous writers of books who deserve mention are James Thurber, Mel Lazarus, Edmund Love, Ring Lardner, Peter De Vries, Clarence Day and Robert Benchley. For humorous poetry you can hardly beat Ogden Nash, Phyllis McGinley and Richard Armour.

Among the columnists for whom it is always laugh time, the names of Art Buchwald and Erma Bombeck stand out. There are several others whose columns in daily and weekly newspapers and in magazines reflect the knowledge that people want to laugh. I suggest that you visit a large university or public library and discover for yourself those columns which are designed to "chisel a chuckle." *The West Virginia Hillbilly* published at Richwood, West Virginia, is a prime example of those once-a-week papers with an editor of considerable humor. *The Hillbilly* calls itself a weakly publication—the choice of "weakly" was no accident. Editor Jim Comstock can laugh at himself and his newspaper. Consequently, he offers cleverly written editorials and dozens of humorous short pieces on "Americana."

Another excellent source of healthy humor is *Sunshine,* a magazet published monthly by the House of Sunshine in Litchfield, Illinois. It costs so little and gives so much. What an investment! Actually, it has become a part of my life, at least of my spiritual and humorous life.

I will not make the effort to identify all the books in my library of humor which teachers should know about, but some do merit special attention. First, there is *The Humor of Humor* by Evan Esar. It was one of the first and best books on humorology in my collection. The publisher is Horizon Press, New York. As an editor, teacher, lecturer and writer I frequently use *The Left Handed Dictionary* by L.L. Levinson, Cromwell-Collier Publishing

Company, and *The Devil's Dictionary* by Ambrose Bierce, Hill and Wang Publishers.

Prentice-Hall, Inc., the publisher of many humorous books, has published a number of books of humor by Chicago Judge Jacob M. Braude. Available from the company is an eight-volume *Complete Speaker's and Toastmaster's Library* by the Judge. Prentice-Hall also published two of my books on school humor, *Teachers' Treasury of Stories for Every Occasion,* 1958, and *Educators' Handbook of Stories, Quotes, and Humor,* 1963. The former is now out of print but still available in most libraries.

In case you don't find what you want in the above sources to start you and them laughing, there are humor services for a fee. Robert Orben runs the mirth mill in his Queens wisecrackery. He not only composes contemporary humor daily, but he also provides a bi-weekly humor newsletter well worth the subscription price. Some of his original humor now appears in book form also. The address is Comedy Center, Inc., 801 Wilmington Trust Building, Wilmington, Del. 19801.

In Indianapolis, Mack McGinnis gleefully puts together a weekly humor newsletter called *Comedy and Comment* which for the most part is a summary of the gleanings of the lighter side of America as expressed by the nation's columnists. The cost is quite reasonable. Mack's address is Mitchener Avenue, P.O. Box 1225, Indianapolis, Indiana.

The weekly digest that grows into a book is a good way to describe *Quote,* the only publication of its kind in the world. This little publication is a weekly compilation of quotes, humorous and otherwise, from the speakers, writers, statesmen, politicians and people in the news from all over the world. A subscription to *Quote* is a very wise investment for any teacher. It doesn't cost, it pays! *Quote* is published in Anderson, South Carolina, Box 4073, 29621.

"Did you make someone laugh today? Why not?" asks George Q. Lewis, Head Jester of Humor Societies of America, 342 Madison Avenue, New York, New York. The guiding principles of the Humor Societies of America are to involve more people in the joy of laughmaking, to encourage the pursuit of happiness, and to discover and develop the future funny people of America. Their motto is "Help put a smile on the map of America." Any teacher who really believes in giving himself and his proteges a lift with a laugh should get in touch with George Q. and the Humor Societies.

Have you seen a teen-age comic lately? Is there one in your school? The fact is there are few youthful comedians or humorists of note anywhere. We educators are partly to blame for that.

Put a smile on the face of America's school children through a teaching style which includes a sprinkling of healthy humor. As I stated, the basic requirements are a willingness to amuse and be amused, and an investment in *Quote, Sunshine Magazine, Comedy and Comment* from *Mack McGinnis, Current Comedy* from Bob Orben in New York, and this book. For an investment of less than $65 a year you can make the humor parade in our schools bigger and better.

THE MANY WAYS TO USE HUMOR IN EDUCATION

We need a regeneration of healthy humor in our society. Since classrooms are miniature societies in a sense, a regeneration of humor there also is desirable. More uncommon than common today are hollow laughs from hollow men.

How well I recall the resounding laughter from the "Liars Bench" in front of the courthouse in scenic Brown County, Indiana. Tall tales grew taller and taller and more incongruous through the practiced imagination of the "stars." That phenomenon is practically gone. Those goofy good times have been replaced with moping. All over America the V sign which meant successively "I want to be excused," "victory" (World War II), and "peace" was lately replaced with the upraised fist. There's little healthy humor in confrontations, vandalism and power struggles, certainly not to the losers and victims—maybe some perverted humor for the victor and the perpetrator.

Man has to survive his adversities and Milton Mayer points out that humor is man's survival kit. Steve Allen suggests that humor is a social lubricant and a humanizing agent. Other sources indicate that humor is a tonic, a sixth sense, a safety valve and an oil for zestful living. I believe them all.

Our students need survival kits. Anyone who understands anything at all about child development and especially the adolescent phenomenon appreciates the social lubricant function of humor. The journey into adulthood is not a velvet-lined path and the need for humor recourse as a tonic, a sixth sense, a safety valve and an oil for zestful living is a critical one for our youth.

A sense of humor is not inherited, like big feet or dimples. It is something to be taught—to be learned. Our time presents a unique opportunity for learning by means of humor. "A perceptive or incisive joke can be more meaningful than platitudes lying between two covers."[19] Even a bad joke is better than none at all.

To some extent at least our doctors are trying out the Chinese art of acupuncture. Another bit of Chinese custom ought to be revealed. According to Wells[20] no part of China's legacy to civilization is more unusual or precious than its singular gift of humor. As all persons acquainted with Chinese statuary are well aware, the Chinese, unlike most peoples, actually created for themselves a god of humor and of laughter.

Our classrooms can stand some kind of symbol, slogan, banner to remind us all that,

> The man who deals in sunshine,
> Is the man who gets the crowds;
> He does a lot more business
> Than the man who peddles clouds.[21]

In his *The Nature of Personality,* Professor Gordon Allport suggested, as I remember it—accuracy is not claimed—that adulthood is more than a matter of mere chronological age. Rather, it is a state in which the human personality is constantly developing, as contrasted to a state of arrest. Certain qualities mark and describe adulthood, among them a sense of perspective, the ability to empathize, and a sense of humor.

Some 12 years ago an Illinois teacher, Wilmer LaMarr, published a pamphlet with an elusive title, but something like *Teachers as Pupils See Them,* as I recall. Here are some representative pupil-authored word pictures of their teachers:

> His caption in the school's "candyland" annual is "Lemon Drop." His attitude on the world is soured. There are only two things in all of God's creation which he reveres: Teddy Roosevelt and the Republican Party. He dislikes teaching; he hates being required to help with extra-curricular activities; he despises

crowds; he abhors church suppers; and he canot tolerate people who disagree with him.

Mr. Business-Like never strayed off the subject. Mr. Business-Like was a great perfectionist and demanded everything his way. He never laughed or allowed us to laugh. If we did, we could be sure of getting an eraser or a piece of chalk thrown at us. From the moment we walked into the room until we left, the subject never strayed from English. This provided a dull hour and one to which few looked forward with anticipation.

She reminds me of a walking mummy, because she never smiles, and looks like she is dead. She wears some of the weirdest dresses; they look like the ones my mother gave to our church to send to foreign countries.

Miss Stoneface is a serious lady who never cracks a smile and expects the same of her students. She believes that a little laughing spoils everything. There should be a lot of seriousness in the classroom, but just a little smile would make a serious matter much more interesting. Does she realize that life is not all work?

In my senior year at high school I entered my English course with a teacher who was a riot. He would begin and end every class with a sterling comment or clever joke. With these jokes he could control the moods and feelings of the class for a whole period.

Take Mrs. Youth for instance; she really wasn't young, but her outlook on life was young. She must have been at least 35, but you felt as if she could understand your problems and feelings as if she were seventeen. She always had a humorous story to illustrate a point or break the monotony. I never worked quite so hard for a teacher as I did for her.

Another teacher that I admire is Mr. J. From all indications, he seems to know his subject thoroughly and how to put it across. He has a wonderful sense of humor and knows how to mix it with the work to keep the attention of the class at all times. No matter what particular subject we are on, he knows how to make the joke that will put his point across to everyone.

His sense of humor smoothed over all the rough edges. When you went into his class, you had a good feeling about school, for he could keep his class in stitches and still teach the lesson and get his points across.

Regardless of most other variables, the teacher does make the difference. And the teacher with humorpower makes an even greater difference. The teacher with the higher humor quotient may find it easier to communicate with youth.

Much of what is called teaching does not teach. Words roll out of open mouths, but the receivers are not receptive. Motivation may be the problem. Sometimes the teacher who "hams" can motivate pupils to "tune in" and learn. "Hamming" is quite common in the theater and in television commercials. Just think for a moment how well young TV viewers know those commercials. They communicate to youth.

Leonard Bernstein's program of music for children on CBS is an example of "hamming." Actually, Bernstein "hammed" his way to successful teaching, for his program from the New York Philharmonic was widely acclaimed as educational and delightful. Bernstein explored musical humor and classified it as wit, satire, caricature, cartoon or burlesque. With varying amounts of practice individual teachers can learn to employ the "hamming" technique to make what they teach understandable and receivable. Bernstein did it. Abraham Lincoln did it. Maybe classroom teachers can do it.

Diagnosis.

In getting to know their learners, teachers are urged to employ multiple data-gathering devices. I believe they should. Before one teaches another, he must first know a great deal about the intended receivers. Although the scholarly books I've read on learner diagnosis generally omit humor, I suggest that such an omission is unjustifiable.

Medical, psychiatric and psychological test data reveal that a healthy sense of humor is closely associated with adjustment to life and intelligence. Research at Ohio State University revealed that one's humor preferences are to a large extent indicative of his personality type. Since humor is an element of both the affective and cognitive functions of the mind, why not at least recognize it as one of many diagnostic tools?

Humanizing.

Thomas Carlyle avowed, "True humor springs not more from the head than from the heart; it is not contempt; its essence is love." In the 70's there appears to be renewed effort to provide teaching-learning encounters which are more humanistic than mechanistic. Humor is human and there is hardly a better way to support humanness than to infect a classroom, a teacher's lounge or a staff meeting with some true humor which delights even as it nurtures.

The deepening struggle between man and mechanism makes a sense of humor doubly important. Any sentimentality about "Americana" ought to include "Save the humor," for it is surely endangered by the present and future shock of chemical and electronic wizardry.

Good humor is contagious to just about the same degree as depression and cynicism. Infectors and carriers are needed in sufficient numbers to reduce an oversupply of dehumanized schools. Use humor to humanize education.

Democratic Living.

It's a sad commentary on American education that rarely does the word humor appear in any form of the materials of learning. On the other hand, the phrase "democratic experiences" is quite a familiar cliché in educational literature. Here's the point. One of the most democratic of experiences is humor. The moment our students laugh together, enjoy exuberance together, and share the medication of mirth, differences of race, background and religion vanish, at least temporarily. In that humor break they are united and equal.

Variety and Unpredictability.

Research says to the teacher there is no one best way to teach. But any one of several good ways to teach always incorporates variety and freshness. The strategic use of humor in educational settings is one way to employ variety. It was Alfred North Whitehead who said, "Knowledge does not keep any better than fish." For your consideration I offer my own wisdom, "Humor does keep better than fish"—which logically must mean that humor keeps better than knowledge.

The educator who wants to infuse the profession with variety and freshness should consider the virtues of humor. His wise use of humor can make him versatile and unpredictable. With versatility there is little danger. Unpredictability is something else. Students thrive on unpredictable teaching methods, yet they need rather consistent expectations to conform to.

Tension Reducer.

More than one principal and more than one teacher have been in dire need of quick and effective ways to cool the school and the classroom. Tensions are produced by all sorts of communications impasses. The ideal that each person is capable of reducing his hypertensions is not yet attainable. Therefore, many occasions arise when it becomes urgent for some kind of "other direction" to intervene for the good of all.

The right kind of humor at the right time has prevented many explosive situations and alleviated others. Educators should develop their own humorpower for tension reduction and encourage it in their pupils.

Openers.

People in show business, advertising, selling and public speaking have learned the value of initiating communications with a bit of humor. When the substance and delivery are fresh and surprising, it works. It's perfectly ridiculous sometimes to observe sober and pompous teachers begin classes. It's no wonder they often start the session with something less than rapture on the part of the pupils.

Opening comments are vital to the communicator and while some experts do it with questions or startling statements of fact, some find the humorous beginning useful.

Creative expression and good timing enable humor to succeed beyond imagination. Remember, too, that it can fail utterly. Nevertheless, it's a good investment of time and energy to create, borrow, store up and practice some light opening remarks. They often function as thought starters. It's a dull moment when there's no whetstone for the wit.

Preoccupied minds.

Communications theory teaches us that receivers are not always ready to accept messages when they are sent and as they are intended. Communicatees screen, block, and sort all kinds of messages reaching their sense organs. One obligation of the message sender is to prepare the recipient to receive the messages as he intended them to be received. When communications fail either the sender or the receiver, or both, may be at fault. When learning fails the same principle holds true for teacher and pupil.

Any aware teacher recognizes that nearly all prospective learners have preoccupied minds. A teacher realizes his obligation to somehow get the pupil to "attend" to the learning situation. In other words, a first principle of teaching is breaking through preoccupied minds.

Two days ago I was lecturing to my undergraduate class. For reasons partially known to me some of them were not "attending" to the moment. They were suffering from the malady sometimes called "astral out-of-body projection." With the young, as with adults, the mind sometimes leaves the body and goes where it will. Purposely, I added to the lecture this preoccupation breaker, "Pardon me for talking so fast, but I can't stand this lecture." The effect was amazing. It brought them back although they didn't really know whether I meant what I said. As a matter of fact, I was asked after the lecture why I said that and if I really felt that way.

Humor is only one way to gain or regain attention, but it is a way. But unless you're absolutely brilliant, don't rely always on your spontaneous wit. Stockpile some attention getters and practice how, where and when to use them.

To Make a Point.

Believe it or not, an ounce of humor is often a more profound "clincher" than a pound of serious explanation. There is much sense in nonsense. It is true that some humor merely produces laughter, but long ago I discovered the cognitive aspect of humor. In short, humor is a great asset to "making a point."

Someone said, "Good teaching is good explaining." It is that, partly. Explanations may require illustrations. That's where humor can help. But what humor? Obviously you can't explain with humor unless you have it ready. Point! Build yourself a file of "point stories." They're available, but you will have to go after them. It works for me. It might work for you.

Holidays and Vacations.

The school year has stops and starts, hills and valleys, and "wow" days and "ho-hum" days. Any given day in the school year for most pupils has its own peculiarities. For one pupil it's getting through that last period. I wonder how many teachers consciously build some variety into their methods to accommodate the above-mentioned variations in the day and year.

Preceding and following vacation periods and big holidays pupils seem to experience considerable difficulty in concentrating on concepts or even understanding simple principles. Teachers are not entirely unaffected either. Such other school happenings as athletic contests and big exams are sometimes destructive to pupil attention span, motivation and morale.

The "bridging" teacher makes honest efforts to help pupils make all their "crossings." My own humor file includes the categories "seasonal humor," "holiday humor," and "report card day shock." Humor in the form of fun games, jokes, quips and anecdotes is quite appropriate for easing transition. Other occasions when the light touch can be implemented include the first snowfall, the first spring day, election day, dress-up day, clean-up day, etc.

The Mischief of Language.

One of my more imaginative teachers in training, Debbie Branam, came up with a novel and potentially effective approach to teaching appreciation for poetry. It employs humor. Here was her introduction:

> The frogs and the serpents each had a football team, and I heard their cheerleaders in my dream:
>
>> *(Boys in the class cheer as follows:)*
>
>> "Bilgewater, bilgewater," called the frog,
>> "Bilgewater, bilgewater
>> Sig, boom, bog!
>> Roll 'em off the log,
>> Slog 'em in the sog,
>> Swamp 'em, swamp 'em,
>> Muck, mire quash!"

(Girls in the class cheer as follows:)

"Sisyphus, Sisyphus," hissed the snake,
Sibilant, syllabub,
Syllable-loo-ba-log,
Scylla and Charybdis,
Sumac, Asphodel,
How do you spell success?
With an S-S-S!"

In the above humorous attempt to motivate an interest in poetry, both concepts and principles of literary devices in sound may be taught. For example, both alliteration and assonance are highly visible in the cheers.

In the following "NEAB Song" one finds use of onomatopoeia, alliteration and assonance:

Snickles and podes,
Ribble and grodes
That's what I wish you.

A nox in the groot,
A root in the stoot,
And a gock in the forbeshaw, too.

Keep out of sight
For fear that I might
Olom you a gravely snave.

Don't show your face
Around any place
Or you'll get one flack
Snack in the bave.

When different students in my class read the "NEAB Song" with emotion, amusement prevailed and some learning resulted, I hope.

In this section we have explored the meaning and nature of humor and indicated some of its functions. The phenomenon of laughter was analyzed and we attempted to relate humor, laughter and joy to learning. Several sources of humor were identified. Finally, we suggested how and when to use humor in the classroom.

Wit and humor of much levity
Communicated with brevity
May have longevity.

REFERENCES

1. Arthur L. Bradford, "The Place of Humor in Teaching," *Peabody Journal of Education.* September, 1964. Used with permission. Copyrighted by *Peabody Journal of Education.*
2. Mark Van Doren, *The Happy Critic.*
3. Horace Walpole.
4. Jacob Levine, *Motivation in Humor* (New York: Atherton Press, 1969).
5. Leo Markham, *The Psychology of Laughter* (Holdeman-Julius Company).
6. Martin Grotjahn, *Beyond Laughter* (New York, N.Y.: McGraw-Hill, 1957). Used with permission.
7. William B. Fry, *A Study of Humor* (Palo Alto, California: Pacific Books, 1963).
8. Jack Condon, "Now Let's Be Serious," *Chicago Daily News.*
9. Sam Levenson, as told to Martin Abrahamson, "Give Your Child the Gift of Laughter," *Family Circle*, February, 1960.
10. Stephen Leacock, *Humor: Its Theory and Technique* (New York: Dodd, Mead and Company, 1935).
11. Albert Cullum, *The Geranium on the Windowsill Just Died But Teacher You Went Right On* (New York: Harlan-Quist Publications). Used with permission.
12. Charles G. Rouscult, *Quote*, October, 1970.
13. M. Dale Baughman, Editorial, *Contemporary Education* (Terre Haute, Indiana: Indiana State University), October, 1969.
14. *The Teacher Paper*, October, 1971, p. 11.
15. *The Instructor*, June 7, 1969.
16. Wilfred Peterson, *This Week Magazine*, February 19, 1961

17. M. Dale Baughman, *What Do Students Really Want?* (Bloomington, Indiana: Phi Delta Kappa Educational Foundation, 1972).

18. M. Dale Baughman, Editorial, *Contemporary Education,* May, 1970.

19. Herbert Marshall McLuhan and Quentin Fiore, *The Medium Is the Message* (New York: Random House, 1967).

20. Henry W. Wells, *Traditional Chinese Humor* (Bloomington: Indiana University Press, 1971).

21. *Fifth Wheel,* House Magazine, Motor Transportation Industry, September 1, 1960.

SECTION **3**

Selections of Educational Humor

―――――――――――――ADOLESCENTS―ADOLESCENCE―――――――――――――

A modern definition of fear: watching your teen-ager drive off in his four-wheel lawsuit!

—John Halla

Adolescence is like a hitch in the Army: you'd hate to have missed it, and yet you'd hate to repeat it.

—*L & N Magazine*

Teen-age girl to girl friend: "He's at that awkward age. He likes to park, but he doesn't know why."

—Bob Goddard, St. *Louis Globe-Democrat*

Did you hear about the teen-ager who plans to run away from home just as soon as she gets a long enough telephone extension cord?

—Art Unger, *Senior Scholastic*

Some members of the younger generation believe that elbow grease is a petroleum product.

—Douglas Meador, *Matador* (Texas) *Tribune*

"Why did you put that 50-foot extension cord on the telephone?"

"Because," said the father, "now that the weather is nice I want my daughter to spend more time outdoors."

—Leo Aikman

When my ten-year-old daughter announced that she was going to put her hair up in pin-curls, I felt a pang of nostalgia, thinking how quickly she was growing up. It was most reassuring to pass

91

the bathroom door a short time later and see her carefully wetting each curl with her water pistol!

—Eugenia Campbell (Frankfort, Ky.)

These young people so indignant about "the establishment" will get over it as soon as they get established.

—Miami Beach *Rote Rays*

A teen-age girl had tough luck in her cooking class at school. She flunked in defrosting.

—*Laugh Book*

The young lad with very long hair entered the barber shop and read magazines. Finally the barber told him he was next. "Oh, I don't want anything," the lad said. "So why did you come in?" "Well, my mother is looking for me and I didn't think she'd look here."

—Clarendon W.

The other day I overheard two fathers in dialogue. "Is your son one of those alienated youth we hear so much about these days?" "I dunno, we don't talk to each other."

—Unknown

There is nothing wrong with the average parents that their teen-age daughter can't exaggerate.

—Lavonne Mathison, *Family Weekly*

A teen-ager had a heart-to-heart talk with his father and said: "Listen, dad, I've come to the decision that it's time for me to stand on my own two feet—but I can't do it with my present allowance."

—Charlie Wadsworth, *Orlando Sentinel*

Fellow called Saturday morning and said he summoned his teen-age son—who is always lifting weights and doing pushups—to him, handed him a shovel and pointed wordlessly to the white stuff covering the sidewalks. "Gee dad," the youth cried, "I can't do that. It builds up the wrong muscles."

—James Dent, *Charleston* (W. Va.) *Gazette*

Father to teen-age son: "Man, it's real cool outside. So why don't you get with it and dig that crazy snow?"

—*Junior Scholastic*

Mrs. Robert B. Richardson Sr. found it necessary to lecture her teen-age son and daughter for going out too much. Unfortunately, just as she had worked up to laying down the line to them, she was interrupted and had to leave the room.

As she was leaving, however, their father was walking into the house, and Mrs. Richardson had an idea that he was going to have a few words to say about over-using the family car.

That's when she heard her son, Robert Jr., remark to his sister: "And now for a word from our alternate sponsor."

> —Paul Crume, *Dallas Morning News*

He: "You're the only girl I've ever loved in my whole life."
She: "Beginners! Beginners! All I ever get is beginners!"

> —Unknown

Despite the hopes of hundreds of singers, the troubles of young lovers are far from few. Take the 12-year-old Memphis lad who met his girl at the movies the other day.

When his mother picked him up later, he was fuming furiously.

"Susie and I broke up," he stormed. "I told her never to speak to me again."

"Why?"

"Why? Because she ate up all my popcorn, that's why."

> —Lydel Sims, *Memphis Commercial Appeal*

Ruth Gillis tells about the sweet young thing who was complaining about a stiff neck and a sore arm after a recent weekend. "How come?" she was asked.

"We were necking in a drive-in."

"Why should that give you a stiff neck and a sore arm?"

"We were in different cars."

> —Forest Duke, *Las Vegas Review Journal*

Kids are getting married younger all the time, and we're expecting any day now to see the bride and groom leave the church on their skateboards.

> —Unknown

Being teen-aged must be awkward. Imagine knowing how to make a phone call but not how to end one.

> —*Changing Times*

A high school student says he'd just as soon take a bus to school as a car, but his dad doesn't have a bus.

—Algoma Record-Herald

A father says his teen-age son took a job-aptitude test: he was found to be suited for retirement.

—Supervision

A young girl describing her strict upbringing: "My parents would let me go to a drive-in theater only in the day time."

—Shotsie, Chicago Tribune

A reader sent in a report of a conversation she overheard recently on 34th Street, in New York, when a visitor stopped two young girls in blue jeans and headbands and asked the way to the Empire State Building. Pointing down the street, one of the girls said: "You can't miss it. It's across the street from the record shop."

—Caskie Stinnett, Holiday

When you watch teen-agers dancing these days, you wonder what they do for relaxation.

—Franklin P. Jones, Quote

A tall, thin teen-ager had been sent to the principal's office for fighting. Asked why she was always getting in fights, she said, "As long as they call me 'Turnpike,' I'll fight."

"But why do they call you that?" exclaimed the principal.

"Not a curve in sight," said the girl sadly.

—Unknown

You know, some of those songs put out by teen-age combos wouldn't be half bad if they were set to music.

—Changing Times

Teen-age brother welcoming sister's suitor: "Come in. She's upstairs spinning her web."

—Shirvanian, Family Circle

> At parties when our boys were small,
> I always had to be on call
> To welcome each arriving guest
> And chaperone the rascals, lest
> They chase each other up the stairs
> And bounce on all the beds and chairs.
> How different from the teen-age crowd!

They make it clear I'm not allowed
Inside the recreation room
Where lights are low and records boom.
They tell me I should disappear
Until refreshment time is near.
They do not want me bright and witty;
They want me on the food committee.
                    —Jean Conder Soule, *Laugh Book*

Sen. Kenneth B. Keating (R—N.Y.) had this letter from the parent of a teen-ager: "Now that my son has a license, I always know where he is. The only trouble is, I don't know where the car is."

                    —Unknown

Danny's father feels strongly that today's children are over-indulged, so he was disturbed when Danny begged to be driven to his school, only three blocks away, because of a light snowfall.

"Drive you to school?" he exclaimed. "Danny, why do you suppose that God gave you two feet?"

"One foot is to put on the brake," Danny answered seriously, "and the other is to put on the accelerator."

                    —Mrs. Rex Campbell, *Catholic Digest*

When John was graduated from high school on his 18th birthday, he found a small gaily wrapped package on the night table in his bedroom. No card was attached and he brought it downstairs and asked his parents who left the package for him.

"Open it and see," urged his mother, smiling.

John tore open the paper and drew out two strips of printed percale. He was baffled for a moment and then realized what they were—his mother's apron strings.

                    —*Catholic Digest*

When our son was a mere baby,
He slept days and was awake nights;
And now that he's a teen-ager,
He's working hard for the same rights.
                    —Giles H. Runyon, *Successful Farming*

Tersh Gentry defines a teen-ager: A boy who has his mother's eyes, his grandmother's mouth, and his father's car keys.

                    —Unknown

Congratulating my son on his 13th birthday, I asked him how it felt to be a teen-ager.

"It's all right, I guess," he replied, "except for the reputation."

—Jim Hewitt, *Catholic Digest, Quote*

Teenager writing home from summer camp: "Send food! All they serve here is breakfast, lunch and dinner!"

—*Rock Hill Herald*

Most teen-agers know the value of a dollar—about two gallons of gasoline.

—*The Wrap-Up*

Excerpt from a letter by a 14-year-old girl reporting to a friend on the gifts she received after graduating from junior high: "And Grandma gave me a diary. It is a nice diary, but it is awfully late to start a diary now. Everything has happened."

—*New Yorker, Quote*

Usually when a teen-ager talks less than half an hour on the phone she has dialed the wrong number.

—T.O. White, *Tow Lines*

As I understand it from studying the stream of high schoolers adorning my living room, adolescence is a time when a boy notices that a girl notices that he is noticing her.

—Burton Hillis, *Better Homes & Gardens, Quote*

I have a 14-year-old boy. His name is Brad. The condition of his room was very, very bad. When I reminded him of his unsightly pad, he said, "Now listen, dad, don't disturb the ecology of my total environment. I don't want to clean it up. I don't want you to clean it up. I know where everything is," and he did—it was on the floor.

Finally, in desperation I gave him $5 and said, "I never want to see your room like that ever again." And I never have. He bought a lock for the door.

—M. Dale Baughman

R.G. Sutherland's definition of teenage togetherness: "Her hair curlers getting caught in his hair curlers."

—Bob Goddard, *St. Louis Globe-Democrat*

The energy of youth increases in direct proportion to the fatigue of parents.

—Unknown

My teen-age girl emerges as a fresh and fragrant bloom, no flaws default the whole effect, but you should see her room!

—Unknown

The speed with which youth can clutter up a house or a room equals or surpasses the rate at which an adult can clean it.

—Unknown

Our 15-year-old son approached his girl friend with one hand cupped over the other. "Kay," he said, "if you can guess what I have in my hand, I'll take you to the show tonight."

"An elephant?" Kay asked.

"Nope, he replied. "But that's close enough. Pick you up at 7:30."

—Eugene A. Thomas

Puzzle for today: Translate the following sample of modern big city talk by teen-agers, groovy teen-agers, that is. Our authority is an Associated Press dispatch:

"Bring your bod over tomorrow and we'll hop in my pig, catch the rays and have a boss time. Everything is freak, baby. My pig can hang a Ralph, hang a Louie, or hang a Ulysses at high speed. If you can't cut it, bag it, man."

Glossary of terms: Bod—body. Pig—small car with powerful engine. Catch the rays—get a suntan. Boss—great. Freak—fine. Hang a Ralph—right turn. Hang a Louie—left turn. Hang a Ulysses—U turn. Can't cut it—can't bear it. Bag it—forget it.

—*Liguorian*

My teen-age daughter's growing up;
Adulthood comes in flashes.
When she's not batting baseball flies,
She's batting her eyelashes.

—Sara A. Jones, *Farm Journal, Quote*

If Booth Tarkington wrote *Seventeen* in this sophisticated age, he would have to title it *Fourteen*.

—Donald G. Bloom

Don McQuillen reports that the ultimate in youth alienation from elders occurred recently when a young man stalked out of a conference on aging, refusing to participate in the process.

—Unknown

Have you heard about the kid who was arrested for extortion?

He was selling protection to school teachers and policemen.

—Mark Beltaire, *Detroit Free Press*

The millionaire's young daughter returned from finishing school, and her father gave her a tour of their new mansion. At the swimming pool they stopped to watch several athletic young men diving and stunting. "Oh, daddy," she exclaimed, "you've stocked it just for me!"

—*Geared Together* (Lewisburg, Pa.)

The man who used to talk about the south forty now has a son who talks about the back nine.

—*Comedy and Comment*

"What is an adolescent?" One who is well informed about anything he doesn't have to study. Someone defined "teenage" as the time in life when girls begin to powder and boys begin to puff. Another parent reported that her daughter, in that delicate transitional stage of life, requested for her 12th birthday a BB gun and a brassiere.

In most discussions involving adolescents it is usually concluded that adolescents are human but the conclusion is never unanimous.

—Unknown

A mind, yes, he has one of those,
But it sometimes comes and it sometimes goes,
And if sometime you should find it gone,
Don't fret, don't fume, don't curse the lack
Just wait awhile, it will be back!

—Unknown

An adolescent is a youngster who is old enough to dress himself if he could just remember where he dropped his clothes.

—Unknown

That's the problem nowadays. Obsolescence is planned and adolescents aren't. I sometimes wonder if Alexander Graham Bell would have invented the telephone if he had had teen-agers in his own home.

—Unknown

Up to age 12 boys are about one year behind girls; during the ages 12 to 17 the boys are gradually catching up; from 17 on it's neck and neck.

—Unknown

How come a boy can unwrap a candy bar while holding a sweater, a basketball, and two books, yet can't put a garbage can cover on straight with two hands?

—Unknown

A downtown merchant reports attending a musical where a youth, his hair brushing his shoulders, sang two songs of protest against technology as threatening the survival of all mankind.

Before he began singing, he plugged his electric guitar into a wall socket.

—Hugh Park, *Atlanta Journal*

A letter to Santa Claus from a high school student said he had tried to be a good little boy all year, but—"the girls won't let me."

—Unknown

By way of Herb Daniels and an old almanac I offer these thoughts for your approbation: School's out and there are sparkling vistas of endless time. If I were 12 I'd climb a tree or ride a bike or shag some flies, or I might go fishing or skip flat stones across the water, or build a hut in an old oak tree. Maybe I'd climb a hill and, buried in the velvet green and grass perfume, I'd dream on clouds and be a cowboy, an astronaut, a pilot, or a ship's captain. I'd perch in a cherry tree and gorge on the sweet red fruit or watch the big guys play ball, or throw sticks for my dog to fetch . . . or get something to eat.

I'd find some pop bottles to trade in at the store; I'd put a penny on the railroad tracks and wave at the engineer. I'd build a dam in a ditch and catch crawfish and have a lemonade stand. I'd count my 200-odd marbles and my baseball cards.

If I were 12, I'd wear my brass-studded cowboy belt and know how to throw a slow curve. I'd sneak into the movies. I'd tatoo my muscle and flex it before the mirror. I'd start a club and we'd hold a circus. I'd throw rocks at a crow, climb the rafters of a new house or maybe dig a cave in an empty field. I'd steal some clothesline and make a lasso. I'd eat some more.

I'd play redlight and ghost my way through the silent sounds of night. I'd stretch out in the cool black grass of night and feel the sky's ponderous weight and wish for things wild and wonderous and unknown. Mostly I'd wish that I were a grown man.

But now—oh, now—I wish I were 12!

When girls get curvier, boys get observier.

—Unknown

A man complained that he can't communicate with his teen-age son: "How can you have a man-to-man talk with someone who's wearing one earring?"

—Quote

This is the first generation of kids that hurry home from school so they can call each other on the phone.

—Comedy and Comment

Father of a high-schooler in an affluent suburb asked, "What did you learn today?"

She said, "I learned that if I don't start getting to school 15 minutes earlier I won't get a place to park."

—Bob Talbert, *Detroit Free Press*

A local radio station was to air a panel discussion for teen-agers, featuring four high school dropouts. Two of them failed to show up.

—Comedy and Comment

Overheard: "I survived World War II, 3 auto accidents, 2 bad marriages, 4 grandchildren, 2 depressions, 13 company strikes, 3 mortgages and a bankruptcy, and some fresh teen-ager tells me: "You don't know what life is all about."

—Comedy and Comment

The younger generation is pretty confusing. Half of them extol the virtues of putting it all together while the other half are busy taking it all apart.

—Quote

The young and the old have the answers. Those in between are stuck with the questions.

—Grit

Today's youth certainly has its problems, like the University of Utah coed who lost a contact lens in her boy friend's beard.

—Changing Times

To keep young, associate with young people. To get old in a hurry, try keeping up with them.

—Quote

There's been a wave of house-breakings out our way. We think thieves entered our daughter's room and ransacked it, but it's hard to tell.

—Changing Times

If thieves had gone into junior's room, they'd still be in there searching for a way out.

—Changing Times

From the autobiography of a senior at Deport High School: "I realize that I am now an adult; and along with this adultery, I must assume new responsibilities."

—Paul Crume, Dallas Morning News

The best way to keep teen-agers at home is to make home pleasant—and let the air out of the tires.

—Marshalltown (Iowa) *Times-Republican*

———————————— ALUMNI—CLASS REUNION ————————————

When Ohio State University recently sent out the usual alumni questionnaire, it received this reply in the box inquiring whether the respondent was married: "No, but watch this space."

—Unknown

Several years ago, Harvard broke off football relations with Princeton. Soon afterwards a Princeton alumni luncheon was held in a midwest city. Each guest rose and gave his name, married or single, and number of children. One man rose and declared himself as follows: "Smith, class of 1902, lumber broker, unmarried, two sons—both at Harvard."

—Laugh Book

No matter how the alumni travel to the game, a lot of them end up riding the coach.

—T.O. White, Tow Lines

The Mountain Ear, published at the Veterans Administration Center at Martinsburg, West Virginia, observes: "Twenty years from now, it's sure going to be a switch when the class of 1974 has a reunion and learns what everybody looks like without beards."

—Bill Gold, Washington Post

After traveling 600 miles to attend the recent 25th reunion of his high school graduating class, a gentleman told friends: "It was like a masquerade party, but when it came time to take off the masks, no one did."

—Bob Talbert, Detroit Free Press

Myrt: "How was your class reunion?"

Marge: "The same old faces—but more new teeth."

                          —Kenneth Nichols, *Akron Beacon Journal*

CHILDREN

Basic Arithmetic: A six-year-old girl informed me that two plus two does not always make four. "Two raindrops plus two raindrops," she pointed out triumphantly, "make a puddle."

                          —James Stewart-Gordon

A double indictment was due the small boy who approached the ticket office of a movie theater one afternoon to buy a ticket. "And why are you not in school?" asked the cashier. "Oh, it's all right," the boy smiled assuringly. "I've got the measles."

                          —Eugene P. Bertin, *Senior Citizen*

Randy Merriman ran a contest that sought kids' answers to the question, "If you could go to the moon, what do you think you'd find there?" A ten-year-old's answer: "A lot of moon men working on a rocket so they could come down to earth."

                          —Unknown

The little boy awoke and happily reached under his pillow for his brand new wrist watch. "Gee," he muttered, "it's almost eight o'clock. If mama doesn't call me soon, I'll be late for school.

                          —Eugene P. Bertin, *Senior Citizen*

Children are like pumpkin seeds. Did you ever try to hold one under your thumb?

                          —Unknown

A Monticello ten-year-old recently developed an interest in music. Naturally when he saw a book in the library entitled "Family Happiness Through Rhythm," he . . . well, he's still trying to figure out what all that stuff has to do with music.

                          —*Minneapolis Tribune Almanac*

Overheard: "The kid who used to get a nickel for taking out the ashes now has a grandson who gets a dime for turning up the thermostat."

                          —Bob Sylvester, *New York News*

The Illinois pastor, Harold B. Walker, tells the story of a little girl playing in the sand alone. A neighbor called over the fence, "Where's your mother?" "She's asleep." "Where's your little brother?" "He's asleep, too." Asked the neighbor, "Aren't you lonesome, playing all by yourself?" "No," said the little girl, "I like me."

—Quote

A minister on meeting a little boy asked, "Sonny boy, who made you?"

"To tell you the truth, " the boy replied, "I ain't done yet."

—R.K. Youngdahl, *Secret of Greatness*

One three-year-old's explanation for being atop a ladder, eating cookies: "I just climbed up to smell them and my tooth got caught."

—Indiana Bell News, Quote

Six-year-old Ricky was having a particularly hard time trying to remember the names of such special days as St. Patrick's day. So I wasn't too surprised when he asked, "Isn't April 1 St. Joke's day?"

—Mrs. Jack M. Bryant

Paul Taubman stopped by the table of a woman and her eight-year-old son at his penthouse club in New York City. The mother boasted about the high marks the lad was receiving in school and told Paul to ask him something. "O.K." said Paul, "What's the plural of rhinoceros?" The youngster hesitated a moment, then shrugged and answered: "Who'd want two?"

—Mitch Woodbury, *Toledo Blade*

————————————————— CHILDREN - PARENTS—————————————————

Said a frustrated young mother as she heard her children crying, and looked over her dirty house, "I sometimes wish I'd loved and lost."

—Rotozark, Springfield, Mo.; *Quote*

A mother very much disliked invasions of her privacy and her personal items. Her five-year-old daughter was inclined to tell family affairs. The little girl was invited to a party so the mother told her before she left, "No matter what questions they ask about your mother and daddy, you are to say you don't know." When the little girl returned home the mother inquired, "Did they ask you any questions?" "Yes," replied the girl. "They asked who my father is and I told them I didn't know."

—Unknown

Some parents help their children with home work. Others have children in accelerated programs.

—T.O. White, *Tow Lines*

One of the biggest troubles with child psychology is that most children don't understand it well enough to explain it to their parents.

—Hugh Allen, *Knoxville News Sentinel*

Heard of the already-tired first grader whose mother set a bowl of alphabet soup before him at supper? He examined his first spoonful with a frown.

"What's the matter?" he demanded. "Can't you let a guy forget school for a minute?"

—Hugh Park, *Laugh Book*

A Bloomington teacher tells of the third-grade boy who took some forms home the first day of school. "What am I supposed to do with these?" the boy's father asked. "Just put an X at the bottom so they don't expect too much from me," the boy replied.

—*Minneapolis Tribune* "Almanac"

Kid down the block ran into the house, jumped across the bed, turned over the TV set, and jumped up on the kitchen table. "Mama, mama!" he yelled, "I made an A in school!" "In what?" asked the mother. "Self-control," said the son.

—Kelly Fordyce,
Indianapolis Sunday Star Magazine

Freddie had just started school and was picking up some very strong language from the other boys. His mother, making efforts to cure him of his cussing, told him, "If you don't stop using bad words, we'll just have to pack your things and send you away."

So for a while Freddie was careful. Then one day he forgot himself and let out a stream of bad words.

"Well," said mother, "you know what I said would happen." And she packed a small suitcase with clothing and a few toys and led him to the door. "Well," mother said.

"Well," said Freddie, "I just don't know where the hell to go."

–Unknown

Two fathers were discussing the future of their children. One remarked, "It is said that we spend more on wild life than we do on child life in this country." The other parent shot back, "I find that a puzzling distinction!"

–Unknown

Psychiatrists who tell parents to spend more time with their children are just trying to drum up business.

–"Today's Chuckle," *T.H. Tribune Star*

One day Tommy skipped school to go fishing. He didn't catch a thing–until he got home.

–T.O. White, *Tow Lines*

The preacher was describing the day of judgment. "Lightning will crackle, " he said, "thunder will boom, rivers will overflow. Flames will shoot down from the heavens. The Earth will quake violently, darkness will fall over the world."

Whereupon a small boy in the front pew piped up to ask his daddy, "Do you think they'll let school out early?"

Sunshine Magazine

A third grader came home from school recently and announced jubilantly that his class had a substitute teacher. "And she has only two rules we have to follow," he said, "Sit down and shut up."

–*Quote*

"So your name is Johny Penny?" the teacher said to make sure of the facts. "But your mother's name is Jones?"

"Yes ma'am," Johny said. "You see, she married again and I didn't."

Bob Jones

After the teacher announced that class pictures would be taken the next day, one youngster went home quite distressed.

"Should I wear my uniform to school tomorrow?"

"Why not?" his perplexed mother responded.

"Well, the teacher said tomorrow they're going to take pictures of the entire student body."

—Sister Ann Corbin, *Quote*

Mother: "Why did you get a zero on your spelling paper?"

Billy: "That's not a zero. The teacher ran out of stars so she gave me a moon."

—*Comedy and Comment*

A six-year-old came home from school in Memphis in such high spirits that his mother asked what had happened.

"I saw my girl today."

"That's nice," she said indulgently. "Did you speak to her?"

He grinned proudly. "No, but I turned three flips."

—Lydel Sims, *Memphis Commercial Appeal*

A modern youngster came home from school and announced excitedly, "They've got a magic record player at our school."

"Magic record player?" asked his puzzled mother.

"Yes, you don't have to plug it into electricity—you don't even use electricity to make it play. All you have to do is wind up a crank."

—Unknown

The seven-year-old came home from school clutching a half-dollar in his hand. "Where in the world did you get that?" asked his mother.

"I found it in school." "But are you sure it was lost?" "I know it was lost, because I saw another boy looking high and low for it."

—Ashley Cooper, *Charleston News & Courier*

Watching his daughter talk to a shopping mall Santa, Wilson Davis sighed, "Just think, this year she's talking to Santa Claus and next year her school wants her in a sex-education course."

—Bob Talbert, *Detroit Free Press*

You folks go ahead and agonize about school busing; when it comes to education my pain is more localized . . . like getting a second grader dressed for school while he's finishing the cereal, counting the kittens and watching something called Tubby and Lester on Television. Father's formula: Grab hold of a button and wait for the buttonhole to come around.

But it's all worth it, isn't it, when he rushes through the door in the afternoon, eager to report to you what he has learned at school: "Daddy! Guess who threw up in class today!"

—Comedy and Comment

"I'm going crazy at home," confided Billy to a classmate in the second grade. "It's my parents. If I make noise, they spank me, and if I'm quiet, they take my temperature."

—Sunshine Magazine

When my neighbor and I were shopping in a department store recently she had her little boy along. Riding the escalator to the next floor down, he asked loudly, "Mama, what happens when the basement gets full of steps?"

—Mrs. Edward Brown, *Grit*

"Daddy," said the little lad, "I went on a class trip today and found out where all the Smiths come from."

"Really?" replied the father.

"Yep," the boy explained. "Over on the other side of town there's a large factory called the Smith Manufacturing Company."

—Quote

U. S. astronauts returned home with 96 pounds of rocks and dirt. But a mother claims her first-grade son still holds the record.

—Knoxville News Sentinel
Editorial, *Comedy and Comment*

The cruelest thing a parent can do these days is to push a bright child through school too fast. What if he arrives at college too young to grow a beard?

—Ohio State Grange Monthly

A nine-year-old boy came home from school and excitedly informed his parents that he knew what his I. Q. was.

"Oh!" his father replied, "How did you find out?"

"My record was on the teacher's desk and I peeked," the son confessed.

"Yes," urged the father, "What was your I. Q.?"

"It was 20-20," proudly stated his son.

—Unknown

A Tulsa father was upset because his wife gave permission for their daughter, who is in the 8th grade, to have a date for a school party. Naturally, he went around making noises as an irate Tulsa father is wont to do.

When the boy showed up, a full six feet in height, good old dad nearly went into orbit. He fumed and foamed all evening, uttering dire warnings to his wife about what he'd do "if anything happens."

Finally on the dot of 9:30 p.m.—when the young Cinderella had been told to be home—there was a telephone call. Both mother and father scurried to answer it. Dad won.

"Daddy," the daughter blurted, "the positively worst thing has happened."

"What did he do?" the father shouted.

"You'll have to come and get me," the daughter said. "His mother came and got him at 9 o' clock."

—Troy Gordon, *Tulsa World*

You heard maybe about the girl who joined the Peace Corps and was sent to deepest Africa. A few months later her mother got a telegram from her which read: "Just got married. Meet me and new hubby at the airport Tuesday night."

Well, mama got all excited and she telephoned the relatives and neighbors, and the next night they drove out to the airport to meet the plane.

It arrived right on time, and the first person to step out was our gal. She was arm in arm with a big Zulu with a ring in his nose, wearing a feathered headdress and loin cloth and carrying a spear and ceremonial mask.

Mama took one frightened look at him, and screamed at her daughter, "No, no, you dumbhead! I told you to marry a rich doctor."

—*Comedy and Comment*

After many years of debate, it is now pretty clear that insanity is hereditary. Parents get it from children.

—*Changing Times*

Wife to husband: "Please take Junior to the zoo."

Husband: "Nothing doing. If they want him, let them come and get him."

—Unknown

A small boy was walking along, crying bitterly.

"What's the trouble, son?" asked a kindly gentleman.

"My mother lost her psychology book," the lad explained between sobs, "and now she's using her own good judgment."

Santa Fe Magazine, Quote

A mother asked her young son to wash his hands and arms. "For long or short sleeves?" he wanted to know.

Grant County (Okla.) *Journal*

Grandmother saw Billy running around the house slapping himself and asked him why.

"Well," said Billy, "I just got so tired of walking that I thought I'd ride my horse for a while."

−Unknown

A father of our acquaintance is flattered by the beaded belt his daughter made for him at camp and thinks he may be able to use it as a watch strap.

−Unknown

"Gee, mom," he complained. "None of the other guys are wearing lipstick." "Shut up, stupid! We're almost at the Draft Board."

−McAlester *Eye Opener*

Two youngsters were walking home from Sunday School after having been taught a lesson about the devil.

"What do you think about all that devil stuff?" one asked.

"Well," replied the other thoughtfully, "You know how Santa Claus turned out. It's probably just your dad."

Quote

While one of his children listened, speaker Ty Boyd of Charlotte, North Carolina, was bemoaning his monthly fate in having to pay all the bills.

While he continued to moan and groan, the child went into the kitchen where mother was working.

"Mommy," the child suggested, going straight to the point, "I think we should give daddy a pity party."

−*Comedy and Comment,*
Mack McGinnis, Indianapolis, Indiana

Three small boys were sitting on the curb, one playing with an airplane, one with a fire engine, and the third reading *Playboy*.

A kindly old gentleman approached and asked them what they wanted to be when they grew up. The first replied that he wanted to be a jet pilot and the second said he wanted to be a fireman. The third looked up from his magazine and mused, "Aw, it isn't important. I just want to grow up."

–Charlie Wadsworth,
Orlando Sentinel, Comedy and Comment

"Brad," screamed mother, "did you fall down with your new pants on?" "Yes, mom," he answered. "There wasn't time to take them off."

–M. Dale Baughman

CLASSROOM SITUATIONS

Teacher: "Who defeated the Philistines?"
Student: "Sorry, but I don't keep track of the minor leagues."

–Unknown

Teacher: "A fool can ask more questions than a wise man can answer."
Student: "No wonder so many of us flunk our exams."

–Unknown

"Does anyone know why a bear sleeps in his cave during the first six months of winter?" the teacher asked her third-grade class.

Eight-year-old Susan waved her hand excitedly. "Yes, Susan?" encouraged the teacher.

"Because there's no one brave enough to go in there and wake him up," Susan explained.

–Tom Haley, *Catholic Digest*

"What parable," a teacher asked a pupil, "do you like best?"
"The one," replied the pupil, "about the multitude that loafs and fishes."

–Unknown

Things hadn't gone well for the third-grade teacher, and she mumbled something only a seven-year-old understands.

A rosy-cheeked, bright-eyed little girl standing near her desk nodded agreement and said in a knowing voice, "Yes, some days just don't go right, and you lose everything—money, marbles and chalk."

—California Education

Teacher: "This is the fifth day this week you've had to stay after school. What do you have to say for yourself?"

Jeff: "I'm sure glad it's Friday!"

—Laugh Book

A teacher was explaining the wondrous things science has discovered about the universe. "Just think," she exclaimed, "the light we need comes all the way from the sun at a speed of 186,000 miles per second. Isn't that almost unbelievable?"

"Aw, I dunno," reported one unimpressed youngster. "After all, it's down hill all the way."

—Society of Automotive Engineers Journal

Teacher: "Can you give me Lincoln's Gettysburg Address?"

Student: "No, teacher, I don't think they numbered houses in those days."

—Unknown

Ted, whose father was a baker, was in the habit of bringing his teacher a fresh pretzel every day.

"I wish you would tell your father not to make them quite so salty," she said once, laughingly.

Thereafter the shiny, brown delicacy, always minus the salt, was found frequently on her desk. "It is very kind of your father to make one on purpose for me," she told Ted.

"Oh, he doesn't make them this way. I lick the salt off."

—Chicago Daily News

The rural school teacher, on the first real cold spell of winter, cautioned her pupils about the dangers of playing on ice-covered ponds and streams. She admonished, "Now, pupils, you must be sure the ice is safe. I had a little brother, only eight years old. One day he went skating on the lake with his new skates. He broke through thin ice and drowned."

After a period of silence, a freckle-faced lad in the back of the room raised his hand and asked eagerly, "Where's his skates?"

—Unknown

A reader tells us about the little girl who ran into her schoolroom and cried to the teacher:

"Two boys are fighting out there, and I think the one on the bottom wants to see you."

—Wes Izzard, *Amarillo Daily News*

A schoolboy came into the classroom long after the bell had rung. When his teacher asked him why he was late, the boy said, "It was so slippery that I took two steps backward for every one I took forward."

"Then how did you get here at all?" asked the teacher.

"I turned around and went home," he answered.

—Alfred Adler, "A Sketch by Elizabeth Hall,"

Psychology Today

Teacher: "Now spell straight."
Small pupil: "S-t-r-a-i-g-h-t."
Teacher: "Correct. Now, what does it mean?"
Small pupil: "Without water."

—*Twentyn* (Norway), *Quote*

A rather stout school mistress was talking about birds and their habits. "Now," she said, "at home I have a canary, and it can do something that I cannot do. I wonder if any of you know just what that thing is?"

Little Eric raised his hand. "I know, teacher. Take a bath in a saucer."

—*Link*

A fourth-grade teacher, discussing heroines from history, asked the class if it knew who Joan of Arc was. "I think," piped a small voice from the rear of the room, "she was Noah's wife."

—*Quote*

Instant definition: Florida State University researchers interested in finding out the "economic concepts" of school children, got this response from one youngster: "Lending money is backwards to borrowing."

—*Quote*

Teacher: "Give me a sentence using the word 'tariff.' "
Boy: "My pants are so tight they'll tariff I bend over."

—*Sunshine Magazine*

It was a bright spring morning and four high-school boys decided to skip classes. Arriving after lunch, they explained to the teacher that their car had a flat tire on the way to school. To their relief, the teacher smiled understandingly and said: "You boys missed a test this morning. Please take your seats apart from one another and get out your paper and pencil."

When the boys were seated, she continued, "Answer this question: Which tire was flat?"

–Rotary Bulletin, Indianapolis, Indiana,

The Rotarian

The College of St. Thomas, much as do other colleges about this time of the year, passes out evaluation forms in which students grade their teachers.

A teacher recently passed out the forms in a business class; after a protracted silence, one student raised his hand and asked, "How do you spell incompetent?"

–*Minneapolis Tribune* "Almanac"

At a public school, a teacher recently asked his ninth-graders to write down three wishes. One boy wrote: (1) I wish I was the richest person in the world; (2) I wish I saw all the Presidents in person; (3) I wish school was out.

–*Comedy and Comment*

The teacher turned to one rather shy little boy and asked him: "Freddie, can you tell me anything about George Washington and Abraham Lincoln?"

"No," said Freddie softly. "We just moved here last summer and we don't know many people yet."

–James Dent,

Charleston Gazette, Comedy and Comment

Word is that the teacher was trying to inspire the members of her class to industry. "Now, children," she said, "there's a wonderful example in the life of the ant. Each day the ant goes forth to work all day. Every day the ant is busy. And in the end, what happens?"

And there came a voice from the back of the room: "Somebody steps on him."

–James Dent,

Charleston Gazette, Comedy and Comment

John was the son of parents who were sufficiently popular to receive more invitations than they could conveniently accept. In the course of a general knowledge lesson, the teacher said, "Can anybody tell me the meaning of the letters, RSVP?"

John's hand shot up. "It means," he explained, "rush in, shake hands, and vanish pleasantly."

Quote

Little Jill's teacher put a picture of Lincoln up on the bulletin board and asked the children who it was.

Several hands went up as Jill blurted out, "Oh, I know. That's the man that makes the pennies."

—Gladys Kent, Lansing, Michigan

"This is where your heart is," said the teacher, pointing to her chest.

"Mine is where I sit down," a little boy called from the back of the class.

"Whatever gave you that idea?" the startled teacher asked.

"Well," the youngster replied, "every time I do something good, my grandmother pats me there and says, 'Bless your little heart.' "

—Edward James Berry

The student asked the teacher, "What's the first lesson in chemistry?" The teacher replied: "Don't lick the spoon."

Omaha World-Herald

COLLEGES—UNIVERSITIES

A student tells us that a dean is a man who doesn't know enough to be a professor but is too smart to be a president.

—Hugh Allen, *Knoxville News Sentinel*

Rex Fletcher knows a lion tamer who turned down a job as college president. Too dangerous.

Comedy and Comment

Speaking at the Catholic Education Association convention in Detroit, the Rev. Theodore Hesburgh, president of the University of Notre Dame, said: "I heard a joke the other day about a university president who died and went to hell and was there four days before he noticed the difference."

Bill Wildhack, *Indianapolis News*

According to Dr. John C. Stephens, dean of the College at Emory, a dean is one-third dreamer, one-third schemer and one-third reamer.

—Leo Aikman, *Atlanta Consitution*

A staff member of a western university was in conference with his dean, who had just mentioned regretfully that his secretary was leaving. Interrupted by a telephone call, the dignified, scholarly dean shuffled through some papers on his office desk as his visitor heard him reply, "I very much liked the young lady you sent over, but I can't place my hands on her form right now."

—James E. Dalley

The freshman dean had dark circles under his eyes. His face was pallid, he wore a hunted expression.

"You look ill," said his wife. "What is wrong, dear?"

"Nothing much," he replied. "But I had a fearful dream last night."

"What was the dream?" asked his wife.

"I dreamed the trustees required that . . . that I should . . . that I should pass the freshman examination for . . . admission!" sighed the dean.

—Unknown

Dr. Elvis J. Stahr Jr., former president of Indiana University, told members of the Hoosier State Press Association he was made to feel like an old-timer in quick time after taking over the I.U. helm.

"About the best way I can sum up these nine months," he said, "is in the words of a colleague who recently introduced me as a speaker and said that my first months of absorbing knowledge about the university and the state must have been like trying to get a drink of water from a fire hose."

—Bill Wildhack, *Indianapolis News*

The president of a small college was visiting the little town that had been his former home and had been asked to address an audience of his former neighbors. In order to assure them that his career had not caused him to put on airs he began his address:

"My dear friends—I won't call you ladies and gentlemen; I know you too well to say that."

—*Arkansas Baptist*

A university English instructor recently introduced to his class what he termed "one of the finest, most elegant lines of poetry in the English language.

"Walk with light," he quoted, and then repeated softly, "Walk with light.

"Now, isn't that a wonderful thing to say to someone?"

The class agreed, of course, and wished to know the author.

"I suppose it's anonymous," said the instructor. "It's written on a sign at the intersection of Main and Ninth Streets."

−Sunshine Magazine

It isn't so bad looking dull and stupid−you don't have to serve on so many committees.

−Dawson County Advertiser-News

A University of Minnesota-Duluth student writes that a classmate, who was more often asleep than awake in class, was nudged by the professor. "I don't mind your going to sleep," the prof said, "but it hurts when you don't say good night."

−Comedy and Comment

Walking down the street with a friend one day, a professor passed a large fish market where a fine catch of codfish, with mouths wide open and eyes staring, were arranged in a row. The professor stopped, looked at them, and, clutching his friend by the arm, exclaimed: "Heavens, that reminds me−I should be teaching a class now!"

−Gene Brown,
Danbury News-Times, Comedy and Comment

While out walking one day, a college professor saw printed on the window of a tiny restaurant: "Lam stew."

The proprietor, standing in the doorway, noticed the professor's smile of amusement and asked for an explanation. He accepted gratefully the professor's lesson in spelling.

The next day the professor passed the restaurant and looked for the window sign. It read: "Clamb Chowder."

−Quote

A college English professor wrote the words "Woman without her man is a savage," on the board, directing the students to punctuate it correctly. He found that the males looked at it one way; the females another.

The males wrote: "Woman, without her man, is a savage."
The females wrote: "Woman! Without her, man is a savage."

–Quote

The law professor was lecturing on courtroom procedure.
"When you are fighting a case and you have the facts on your side, hammer on the facts. If you have the law on your side, hammer on the law."
"But what happens if you don't have the facts or the law on your side?" asked a curious student. "What do you do then?"
"In a case like that," said the professor, "hammer on the table."

–Quote

Outside a lecture hall at Shelton College, Cape May, New Jersey, there is a row of hooks with a notice above reading: "These hooks reserved for faculty members only."
Underneath a line of graffitti has been scrawled: "May also be used to hang up hats and coats."

–Baltimore Sun, Comedy and Comment

The history professor was lecturing about the early days of colonization in this country. "When the pioneers started to settle this country," he began, "the Indians were running things pretty much their own way. There was no air pollution, no smog, no water pollution from city wastes. Taxes were unheard of. There was no such thing as a national debt. The land was free; and, when one place failed to produce a living for the tribe, the Indians simply moved to a more productive spot. Among the Indians, too, the women did all the work and the men were regarded as being the important ones. Are there any questions?"
A student raised his hand. "Please, sir," he asked, "how did the pioneers think that they could possibly improve on a system like that?"

–Quote

A disillusioned professor has urged that every student be compelled to take a basic course in English, "So he'll know another language besides his own."

–Machinist

"I'd just love to have a diamond to go with my new gown you bought me for the faculty dinner," said the professor's extravagant wife. "Do you suppose you could get me one for our anniversary that falls on the same day?"

"My dear," the professor replied, "inexplicable circumstances, perforce, preclude the eventuality of my endowing you with such an estimable bauble."

"I don't get it!" she said.

"Precisely."

−Quote

Problems in Grantmanship:
(An Historical Review Documented by Files from the United States Bureau of Education and Obfuscation)

Dear Mr. Adam:

I regret to inform you that while your project sample population of one seems to qualify as culturally deprived (low purchasing power, lack of proper clothing, restricted diet), it is still a very small N. Could you somehow increase the size of the population?

Sincerely yours,

Dear Mr. Columbus:

The office does not fund projects in which loss of major equipment purchased under grant funds seems so highly probable. However, since the project seems to have some merit, I am enclosing the name of a private philanthropist. If the proper approach is made, this person might give you her support.

Sincerely yours,

Dear Mr. Jenner:

We encourage you and your cowpox project. If you will agree to use only undernourished cows (very thin cows will also be appropriate), the entire project may be allowable under a new title just authorized. Since the funds are to be completely spent in the next 30 days, we will immediately establish an age-weight-underprivileged cow ratio. References you cited from Leeuwenhoek, Kock, Lister, and Pasteur were incomplete. Will you please list by each of the above names (1) where the person did his graduate work, (2) his GPA, (3) his academic rank, (4) his major addresses, (5) the title of his dissertation, and (6) any civic organizations to which he belongs.

Sincerely yours,

Dear General Custer:

Your letter requesting immediate military assistance was misdirected to our offices in H.E.W. Unfortunately, due to major reorganization of the office, the letter was misplaced and not forwarded for several months. We trust this slight oversight did not cause you any undue inconvenience.

Sincerely yours,

Dear Uncle Wilbur and Uncle Orville:

Your idea just won't fit into any of the current research and demonstration programs in my agency. However, if you wish to try other agencies in Washington, here are a few tips: (1) Use scientific terms difficult to understand; (2) make up several new terms no one could possibly have heard of before; and (3) set ridiculous goals. Your proposal to attempt flying in the air around Kitty Hawk may be wild, but I would include flying in the air around the moon as well. Don't take my suggestions lightly. Congress itself may support your project if you confuse them as I have suggested.

Your Nephew,

Dear Mr. Dewey:

Your innovative proposal for a new educational setting seems well thought out and well organized. Chaining both of the student's ankles to the floor and clamping his head in an iron frame so that his eyes can only focus on the book in front of him would seem to be a plan with merit. However, since the President and the iron and steel companies are presently involved in a discussion over price increases, it seems unlikely that any new educational plan that would have schools making major purchases from these industries would be authorized. We suggest you alter a few points in your plan and resubmit.

Sincerely yours,

P.S. A man with a background in physical education and recreation will soon be doing the initial reading of proposals in this area, which may suggest to you possible implications for the tone of your revised proposal.

Dear Mr. Einstein:

Our panel of experts read your proposal for research and the supporting theory. Since we had difficulty understanding the theory, we suggest you call in a consultant who could state your thoughts more succinctly. May we remind you that an idea is of no value unless it can be easily communicated.

Sincerely yours,

Dear Mr. Larson:

Thank you for your submission of a most interesting research proposal. It was sent out for reading to six experts at six major universities. Unfortunately, in each case the expert felt your college was not sufficiently well prepared in faculty and resources to handle such a project. However, assuming the topic and research design you proposed is still of interest to you, you will be pleased to know that we have funded six major universities to work on the problem you suggested. Please continue contacting us for possible support on other ideas you might have.

Sincerely yours,
—Keith H. Larson

Professorial Upmanship.

With the educational prophets predicting an excess of college and university teachers for the coming decade this writer felt compelled to exhort his fellow teachers to engage in the practice of "Upmanship." Upmanship, briefly defined, is the ability to outdo others by any means available, be it fair or foul. Upmanship may also be defined as the ability to retain one's position, regardless of ability, when competing with the ever increasing numbers of bright young Ph.D.'s coming out of the graduate institutions. Hopefully, the following brief suggestions will enable one to get started on the road to superior upmanship:

1. Write each and every book company requesting any and all books remotely associated with your area. This guarantees a full bookcase in the office and impresses students and faculty alike with your intellectual attainment. A caution, however—they are burdensome to move.

2. Always speak out at faculty meetings, especially if the president of the university or an upper echelon administrator is in attendance. Speaking out insures recognition, especially helpful if attendance is being taken. To exercise upmanship of the highest quality, make sure your statements agree with those expressed by

the administration. It is also an especially good technique to interpret to the administration what others have been saying. For example, you might speak up with something like, "What Bill means is . . ." or "What John is attempting to say is that . . ." This technique also wins friends among those for whom you interpret.

3. Post an impressive list of office hours and send copies to all administrators. Of course, you must disregard the posted hours if they interfere with your coffee break(s) or your personal desires. If you are apprehended missing your hours, a good excuse is that you were at the library writing a research proposal.

4. In order to obtain high visibility on campus, volunteer to hold office in as many professional and faculty organizations as possible, regardless of holding paid-up membership or not. A word of caution, though: be sure that the office requires a minimum of effort and a maximum of visibility.

5. Work diligently to attain a high level of ineptness. This insures no tasks being assigned of any importance. If you have any real aptitude for ineptness you can really foul up the first major committee assignment. This will guarantee your future and preclude the chances of your ever receiving any assignments of note or importance.

6. A few words about your efforts in the classroom. Let's face it, teaching just isn't very well rewarded, as research is the currency in the professional realm. Spend your time writing and researching.

7. Back to the textbooks. Check at the bookstore to see what texts they stock, then write the publishers requesting the books of your choice. Then the master stroke: after receiving the textbooks trade them in at the bookstore in exchange for due bills or credit. This technique will give you a massive credit from which you can furnish your office to the envy of all. You can flaunt such cherished items as staplers, hole punchers, notebooks, etc., all purchased from your credit at the bookstore.

8. To really be an upsman one must dress the part. Work to achieve that certain rumpled or disheveled look. Clothing may be purchased at Goodwill and Salvation Army stores, though in some locales the selection may be better at Army and Navy Stores. In order to achieve the proper look one must be ready to spend nights de-creasing trousers and staining ties.

In conclusion, upmanship cannot be achieved overnight, or even in a single academic year. It may take years of practice before one reaches the pinnacle of success. Hopefully, with proper practice and use of the aforementioned suggestions, and with the proper research model, one can become a true academic upsman.

–Sam F. McClanahan, *Contemporary Education,*
published by Indiana State University. Used with permission.

Bill Burson, Georgia's capable and conscientious welfare director, told about Robert Frost as a college professor. Bill said the great Frost did not like to give examinations. On a final, he asked one question, "What did you get out of this course?"

One boy answered, "I didn't get a dam thing." Professor Frost gave him a 90 on the answer. A fellow faculty member asked why the grade was not 100.

"I couldn't give him 100," Frost explained. "He left the 'n' off 'damn.' "

Leo Aikman,
Atlanta Constitution, Comedy and Comment

Among male haircuts featured by some of the 1,000 clippers at the National Barber Show here Monday is the "Economy Prof Cut" for "underpaid but proud college teachers."

–Unknown

A college professor and a farmer were traveling together and decided to ask each other riddles to pass the time.

"When I miss a riddle, I'll pay you a dollar," the professor said, "and when you miss one, you pay me a dollar."

"That's not fair," said the farmer, "you're better educated than me. You pay me a dollar and I'll pay you 50 cents."

The professor agreed to this handicap and the farmer asked the first riddle: "What is it that has three legs when it walks and two when it flies?"

Not knowing the answer, the professor handed a dollar to the farmer, who explained that he did not know the answer either, and handed back 50 cents.

–Jim Henry, *Laugh Book*

A professor who had a Ph.D. degree recently wanted to make an airline trip but found that the reservations were all sold out. So he called the airline's office and said he was Dr. So-and-So and had to make an emergency trip to Boston. After some hesitation on the other end of the line, the passenger clerk asked, "Are you a medical doctor?" The Ph.D. answered that he was "an obese schizophrenic." The clerk thought for a moment, turned to an associate and said that he had an important doctor on the line who had to get to Boston immediately. They placed him on the next flight. When his wife told him he might get himself in trouble, the professor replied, "I doubt it. At least not for calling myself a fat madman."

—United Mine Workers Journal, Quote

When I joined the staff of the University of Illinois fresh from earning my doctor's degree at Indiana University, I was a bit unsure of myself and apprehensive about my contributions to education. One staff veteran of many campaigns comforted me: "Now, Dale, you're likely to be nervous at times but bear up. When I first became a college professor, I too was completely overawed and confused. Then one day a wise old professor took me aside, patted me on the back and said, 'Son, don't worry! The first six months you're here you may wonder how you made it. During the next six years, you'll often wonder how the rest of us made it.' "

—M. Dale Baughman

I knew a university anesthetist. His lectures put the whole class to sleep.

—Paul Light, *St. Paul Pioneer-Press*

"Where is the car?" demanded his wife, as the absent-minded professor came up the front steps.

"Dear me!" he exclaimed. "Did I take the car out?"

"You certainly did. You drove it to town."

"How odd! Now I remember—when I got out of the car, I turned to thank the gentleman who had given me the lift and wondered where he had gone."

—Unknown

A college mathematics teacher was struck by a hit-and-run driver, and the policeman asked him whether he got the license number. "No," the professor replied, "but I did notice that if it were doubled and then multiplied by itself, the square root of the product would be the original number with the integers reversed."

—John Shotwell

Literature Professor: "An anonymous person is one who does

not wish to be known." A few minutes later, stopping his discourse, he said: "We can't have this! Who is causing the disturbance back there?"

Voice: "An anonymous person."

—Unknown

Soviet teachers report partial success in a mass experiment in teaching English to students while they sleep.

That coincides with the results many American professors have been getting for years.

—*Atlanta Journal* Editorial

For helping my wife in the kitchen I have little reputation. However, on a few occasions during my six-month sabbatical leave, I did perform some minor duties in that area of the house.

I was amused one day to discover that my desk nameplate which I had brought home at the beginning of the leave period was conspicuously placed near the sink.

—Unknown

It was breakfast time at the house of the eminent professor, who had spent the major part of the night in his laboratory.

"My dear," he said to his wife, "congratulate me! I have discovered a gas of hitherto unheard-of density, and I'm going to name it after you!"

—Unknown

The first assignment given to the freshman English class at a large university was to write a theme. The professor did not specify a subject since his purpose was to determine his students' ability to spell, their vocabulary, sentence structure and the like.

One coed's paper read in part ". . . the lady was descending the stairs when she tripped, fell and lay prostitute on the floor."

The professor circled the incorrect word with a red pencil and wrote the following note on the margin of her paper: "My dear young lady, you must learn to distinguish between a fallen woman and one who has temporarily lost her balance."

—L.B. Kohler, *True*

Did you hear about the biologist whose research project was changing the behavior patterns of rodents? Whenever he was questioned about the nature of his work, he replied: "I pull habits out of rats."

—Eddie Hilton, *Parade*

The professor of chemistry was giving a lesson on the powers of different explosives.

"This," he explained, "is one of the most dangerous explosives of them all. If I am in the slightest degree wrong in my experiment, we are liable to be blown through the roof. Kindly come a little closer, so that you may follow me better."

—Laugh Book

A philosophy professor urged his students to be tranquil and at ease always. He explained that the secret lay in not letting little things bother one. While he was talking an insect began buzzing around his head and some of the students tittered.

"This fly buzzing around me illustrates my point," said the professor. "It bothers some of you, but it does not disturb me. I am not flailing my arms around in the air trying to get rid of it. I simply ignore it and know it will go away."

About this time the insect settled down on the professor's nose. This was a little too much even for him and he made the slight concession of trying to brush it away with one finger.

Suddenly he leaped to his feet and clutched his nose, "Why didn't one of you tell me it was a bee?" he shouted.

—Sunshine Magazine

The professor stepped up on the platform and, by way of breaking the ice, remarked: "I've just been asked to come up here and say something funny."

At this point, a student heckler in the back of the hall called out: "You'll tell us when you say it, won't you?"

The professor answered: "I'll tell *you*. The others will know."

—Quote

A professor who had taught for many years was counseling a young teacher. "You will discover," he said, "that in nearly every class there is a youngster eager to argue. Your first impulse will be to silence him. I advise you to think carefully before doing so. He probably is the only one listening."

Wall Street Journal

At a professor's housewarming it was apparent to all of us that his luxurious new house, located in an exclusive neighborhood, was in the higher-price bracket. In fact, one of the guests wondered out loud just how a university professor could afford such a layout.

"You will observe, " explained the professor, "that this house is built on a prominent bluff—and it's being paid for the same way."

—Robert F. Hancock

When my husband, a biology teacher, accepted an offer to teach in another city, we had to pack, in addition to the usual household paraphernalia, dozens of cartons of teaching materials—plant specimens, fossils, skeletons.

On moving day I saw one workman grab a box and start to give it the *one, two, three, heave* treatment.

"Oh, please be careful!" I cried. "Those are my husband's bones!"

The workman stopped, still holding the box in mid-air. Then very gently he set it down and, in a quavering voice, asked, "Which husband?"

—Evelyn B. Ridder, La Puente, Calif.

Dr. Eugene Winograd, psychology professor at Emory, commenting on memory, tells the story of a noted professor of ichthyology (study of fish) at an Ivy League University who stopped learning the names of his students because "every time I learn a student's name, I forget the name of a fish."

Leo Aikman, *Atlanta Consitution*

It is said that Woodrow Wilson, when teaching at Princeton, would stride into his classroom, greet the class, and then say, "Gentlemen, are there any questions?" If no questions were asked then the class would be dismissed, since it was Professor Wilson's contention that his young scholars had not prepared for the class that day.

Jesse Burt,"Socrates May Have Been Right,"
Adult Leadership, Quote

While attending the national convention of secondary school principals one year, I had lodgings in the headquarter's hotel in Philadelphia. Being housed on the 14th floor I was a rather regular user of an elevator operated by a wide-eyed and well "made-up" young lady in proper hotel-uniform attire.

On one "up or down" occasion she asked of me, "Are you a professor?" My affirmative answer seemed to give her the opportunity to remark, "I never went to school beyond the fifth grade. I was raised in the backwoods of Tennessee. But I have a cat named Professor."

When I asked, "Why did you name the cat Professor?" I received a most interesting reply. "Well, he has whiskers, he grows by degrees and always seems to be looking for something."

—M. Dale Baughman

Every year, I ask Santa for a Camaro and every year he brings me a can of STP for my Corvair.

—Bill Copeland, *Sarasota Journal*

An intellectual university student decided to write a thesis on a provocative subject: "Psychoanalytical Synthesis of the Application of Ecological Transcendentalism to the Motivation and Behavior Patterns of Adolescent Females."

In other words, "How Girls Grow Up."

—Unknown

Rosalie was in her first semester at college when her mother received from her a special delivery airmail letter reading:

"Dear Mother: Please let me have $35 for a new dress right away. I've had six dates with Johnny and have worn each of the dresses I brought with me. Have a date next Monday night and must have another dress right away."

Her mother replied via Western Union: "Get another boy friend and start over."

—*NRTA Journal*

"Well, since Tom has a college degree, can you see any change in the way he plows?" asked the first farmer.

"No," answered the second farmer, "he plows the same. It's the way he talks."

"Yeah? How do you mean that?"

"Well, when he gets to the end of the row, instead of saying 'Whoa, haw, gee,' he says, 'Halt, Rebecca, pivot and flare out.' "

—*Atlas News,* Atlas Finance Company

The college president was disciplining an unruly student. "I am told," he said, "that you have a barrel of beer in your room."

"Doctor's orders, sir," was the reply; "He said if I drank a lot o' beer I'd get my strength back."

"H'm—and did you?"

"Absolutely! When that barrel came in, I could hardly budge it; and now I can roll it all around the room!"

—*Sunshine Magazine*

"Dad, when I graduate I'm going to follow my literary bent and write for money."

"Son, you ought to be successful. That's all you have been doing since you started college."

—Unknown

A couple of college kids were talking within our area about future hopes and past follies.

"There is no way," said one, "that I can ever persuade that guy to give me a good grade. He still thinks that he's smarter than I am."

—Comedy and Comment

"I've got an idea," said the freshman. "Beginner's luck," said the sophomore.

—Fun Foundry

Tom, a medical student, spent his summer working in a variety of ways to help finance his education. At one time he assisted a butcher in a meat market by day and was a hospital orderly at night. Both jobs required the wearing of similar white uniforms. One evening he was assigned to push a patient, reclining on a stretcher, into surgery. The apprehensive woman looked at Tom, looked again and screamed, "My God! It's my butcher!"

—Betty Ware

Journal of American Medical Association, Quote

Freshman Bloopers.

Despite claims of educationists that education is better than ever in this country, considerable evidence could be garnered from freshmen college papers which would dispute the contention. Any teacher who has had access to the literary outpourings of beginning collegians would be able to provide extensive documentation which would indicate that many students cannot understand what they read, or compose intelligent sentences which express what they think, and—perhaps above all—cannot spell.

For some time, I have composed my own blooper list, items being lifted from the papers of unsuspecting students. Perhaps bringing such errors to public notice is unfitting behavior on the part of a conscientious teacher who should—above all things—try to minimize or hide the ignorance of the pupils entrusted to her care. But since the attempt is not to ridicule, but to illuminate, perhaps the disclosure is permissible.

I confess to taking a sly delight in the spelling of *Episcopalian* which emerges from student writing. It is impossible now to recall the occasion for the use of such a word, but the record shows that in less than five years of teaching, the word has been listed as *Ephiter, Espicalpalian, Espictocal, Episcoplain, Episcipal* and *Eposticalian.* Could Henry the Eighth have dreamed what he was starting?

Suspension, a word fraught with unpleasant connotations, has been defined as "Dispension from school." On another occasion, it was "exspellment," which acquedemically would be embarrassing even for those Eposticalians previously mentioned.

And harking back to Henry the Eighth, would you believe that "the Puritans condemded the drama because of it's wickness." This was done, no doubt, because "the Puritian way of life was very ridge."

Occasionally one is shocked by the table manners seen in public. I have been less so since quizzing students on an etiquette unit. When the question was asked concerning whether elbows are ever permitted on the table, the answer shot back on a paper was: "Yes, during intercourse."

The writing of student autobiographies is recommended for the insights it gives into the personalities of the students. One student wrote a long paragraph on the people she had taken for granite in her life. Another was religiously motivated and declared, "Yes, I am the Lone Ranger, and my Tonto is God!" A third struck home—perhaps unknowingly—when she said, "It never occurred to me until I started thinking about it just how much my family, friends and environment has contributed to the warping of my personality."

A girl was relating an experience she had while spending the night with a pianist friend. "And I heard her, as I fell asleep, struggling with Bach." Is no one sacred?

The teaching of syllogisms to unsophisticated students, meeting elementary logic for the first time, produces the most astonishing conclusions—all delivered in dead seriousness.

> She likes horses.
> All people like horses.

Therefore, she is a horse.

All people have hair.
She is a person.
Therefore, a person is a people.

All dogs have fleas.
My cat has fleas.
Therefore, my cat is a dog.

A literature unit evokes such remarks as that Elizabeth Barrett and Robert Browning were immoralized as perfect lovers. Shakespeare's *Ballad to a Dark Ladie* brought forth the question as to who the Negro might be.

Yet it is student creative attempts which perhaps yield most notable results. A mother, giving vent to personal grief, "gathered her child in her arms and began sobbering." Equally distraught, a boy was unhappy at how a football game was progressing and "a lustful groan came from the bench." A fictional heroine had been consoled by a solicitous beau. "Drew had been so kind, and so understanding, that it had relieved the terrible ache in her barren womb."

Sex always seems to rear its head in student writing. A student was outlining a term paper she proposed to write on polygamy. (Why stick with monogamy when there are such exciting alternatives?) One heading in the outline was: "The position of the wife in relation to the husband." Innocence, it's bliss.

Waxing philosophic, another neophyte writer was bringing in a Biblical parable for emphasis. "The prodigal son tried living on an animal level, but eventually his longing for home destroyed all possibility of happiness in a hog-pen."

All in all, it's great sport, this pedagogical routine. And thank heavens for the bloopers which provide comic relief when the piles of papers might otherwise be more than one could stand.

—Ann T. Bass, *Contemporary Education*

Have you heard about the college student who became hysterical during a demonstration? He burned his credit card by mistake.

—Alex Thien,
Milwaukee Sentinel, Comedy and Comment

"Four long years of college," sighed the girl graduate, "and who has it got me?"

—*Today's Chuckle*

Friend: "So your son left college because of poor eyesight?"

"Yes," answered the father, "he mistook the Dean of Women for a coed."

—Armstrong *Trap Magazine, Quote*

Coed on shopping tour: "Where can I get some silk covering for my settee?"

Floor Walker: "Lingerie—next aisle and to the left."

—Unknown

Professor: "See here, what did you mean by walking out of my lecture this morning?"

Student: "I'm not sure just how it happened, sir. I think I must have been moved by what you were saying."

—Unknown

My thesis is coming along fine—a delicate blend of the obscure, the opaque, and the irrelevant.

—Unknown

A farmer was asked if he missed his boy since his return to college.

Farmer: "I sure do. He got the cows so they wouldn't come home until he gave 'em a college yell and I can't remember it."

—Unknown

The professor of English was trying to drum into his class the importance of a large vocabulary. "I assure you," he said, "if you repeat the word 10 or 12 times, it will be yours forever."

In the back of the room a cute coed took a deep breath and whispered, "Robert, Robert, Robert."

—Unknown

A zoology major was told to provide an exhaustive study about fleas. He laboriously trained a medium-sized flea to jump over his finger every time he said "Hupp." Then he pulled off two of the flea's six legs. "Hupp," he grunted. The flea jumped over his finger. Off came two more legs. "Hupp," repeated the student. Again the flea jumped. Then he pulled off the flea's last two legs. Alas, the flea no longer moved. The student nodded sagely, and wrote in his report: "When a flea loses all six of its legs, it becomes deaf."

—*Pelican*

A crowd of school girls, college students, were riding on a train. One of them who desired to impress the conductor with her education noted a small amount of water on the floor in the aisle between the seats, so she called to the conductor:

"Oh, conductor, have one of your porters remove that H_2O from the floor, please."

"Are you a college student, young lady?" asked the conductor.

"Why, yes, I am," replied the girl.

"Well, I just want to set you straight," the conductor smiled. "That is not H_2O down there on the floor. That is K_9P!"

—Unknown

From one who signs himself as "modern youth" comes the puzzled observation: "While home from college I like to take my parents out to a movie, but the problem is to find one which is the type of thing which parents should see."

—Clyde Moore, Columbus Dispatch

The neighbor's college kid got it all wrong again and came home for home-coming.

—*Comedy and Comment*

On a college birdwalk our instructor identified the first birdcall. When the next call was heard, he asked, "What was that?"

"A chipmunk," one of the girls volunteered.

"No," the instructor said patiently. "That's a tufted titmouse."

"Well," said the girl proudly, "at least I knew it wasn't a bird!"

—Susan Grove, (Northridge, Calif.)

Most college campuses are getting so crowded that if a student wants to be alone, he has to go to class.

—John Gillespie, *Quote*

Freshman: "Say, what is the idea of your wearing my rain-coat?"

Roommate: "Well, you wouldn't want your new suit to get wet, would you?"

—*Sunshine Magazine*

Couple applying for extension of son's college loan: "We had his board and tuition figured out right, but we didn't count on bail."

—*Quote*

Will Rogers' wit was already well developed when the beloved humorist was a college freshman. At college during one of his first classes, the teacher asked him, "Where are your books?"

"I ain't got none," replied Will.

"What would you think of a man going to work without any tools?" demanded the teacher.

"I'd say he was the boss," quipped Will.

Allied Youth, Quote

There are 200,000 useless words. This accounts for college yells.

−Today Chuckle

College is different because it makes you wrangle more with yourself.

−Russel Brantley, *The Education of Jonathan Beam* (Macmillan)

A doctor says if you eat slowly you'll eat less. That is certainly true around a college boarding house.

Emporia (Kansas) *Gazette*

"The college I went to has turned out some great men."

"When did you graduate?"

"I didn't graduate. I was turned out."

−Dawson County *Advertiser, Comedy and Comment*

The Educational Supplement of the *Times* of London recently reprinted without comment the following caution sent undergraduates at King's College, Cambridge: "Gentlemen may be disposed to allow that a modest pride in the appearance of the College is not an entirely obsolete virtue, and therefore that nocturnal exploits which involve disfiguring the lawns with unsightly lines or designs are to be eschewed."

−Unknown

Jones: "How is your son getting on at college?"

Smith: "He must be doing pretty well in languages. I've just paid for three courses—ten dollars for Latin, ten dollars for Greek, and a hundred dollars for Scotch."

−Unknown

Then there was the father who wanted his son to have the opportunities that he never had, so he sent him to a girls' college.

−Jack Herbert

Fall phenomenon: Some students fly to college, some take a train, and some get there by a football coach.

−Today's Chuckle

A young man had just finished his tour of duty and had been released from the Air Corps and had entered the fall semester of a western university. One morning he was about ten minutes late to his nine o'clock class and the professor, knowing that he was on the G.I. Bill, bawled him out in front of the class.

"When you were in the Air Force and came in late like this," said the professor, "what did they say to you?"

"Well, when I came in late," answered the young man, "they just said, 'How are you this morning, colonel, sir?' and stood up and saluted."

—Dan Bennet, *Quote*

How to do it—an eastern university noted for its graduate school of business has begun the school year with an $11 million deficit.

Comedy and Comment

Many a man who was educated at a little red schoolhouse has a grandson being educated at a college that is running in the red.

—*Comedy and Comment*

A member of the faculty of the University of Wisconsin tells of some amusing replies made by a pupil undergoing an examination in English. The candidate had been instructed to write out examples of the indicative, the subjunctive, the potential and the exclamatory moods. His efforts results as follows:

"I am endeavoring to pass an English examination. If I answer twenty questions I shall pass. If I answer twelve questions I may pass. God help me!"

—Unknown

It strikes us that in their dealings with each other, the world's diplomats are like a college prof we once had. At an examination he announced: "This exam will be conducted on the honor system. Please take seats four seats apart and in alternate rows."

—Sam A. Darcy, "The Corner Aphorist," *The Idler*

Bulletin board humor posted at the University of Omaha: "Happiness is sitting behind a round-shouldered student who has the answers to the finals."

—Robert McMorris, *Omaha World-Herald*

The minister, named Jordan, had a son at college. The son was about to take his final examinations and naturally his father asked the boy to let him know as soon as possible how he got on.

In a few days the father received a telegram which read: "Hymn 254, verse five, last two lines."

Looking up the reference in the hymn book he read, "Sorrow vanquished, labour ended, Jordan passed."

—Capper's Weekly

A professor friend of mine recently received an examination paper from one of his more philosophical students. It read in full: "After serious reflection, I have concluded that there is both truth and beauty in these examination questions. The truth is that I don't know the answers and the beauty is that I don't give a damn."

The professor, not amused by this, added the remark, "Ergo Flunkis."

—Quote

A communication from the University of Colorado's news service:

"The school dropout problem took a new twist at the University of Colorado last week. A student's lesson in a correspondence course came back.

"In one corner was a post office stamp. 'Return to Sender . . . Moved—Left No address.' The student was an inmate of the State Penitentiary at Canon City.

"In the other corner the warden had penciled a notation: 'Escaped.' "

—Jack Guinn, *Denver Post*

A college education is a process whereby the notes in the professor's notebook get into the student's notebooks without going through the head of either.

—Unknown

I'm well educated, 'tis easy to see; the world's at my feet for I have my A.B. M.A. will come next, then, of course, Ph.D. But I'd chuck it all for a good J.O.B.

—Sunshine Magazine

Overheard: "I thought working my way through college was tough until I started working my son's way through!"

—Comedy and Comment

At the end of the first week away from home on a new job a young husband wrote to his wife: "Made foreman—feather in my cap."

After the second week he wrote: "Made manager—another feather in my cap."

After the third week he wired: "Sacked—send money."

His wife telegraphed back: "Use feathers. Fly home."

—Funny Girl (*Ottawa Journal*)

A big three-degree man got his first degree from Harvard, his second degree from Yale and the third degree from the Bureau of Internal Revenue.

—*Today's Chuckle*

I'm reminded of the boy who said, "Dad, what do they mean by college-bred?" And the father replied, "College-bred, son, comes from the flower of youth and the dough of old age."

—Leo Aikman,
Atlanta Constitution, Comedy and Comment

My alma mater, good old Baker U., Baldwin, Kansas, has remained relatively calm throughout this time of protest on the campus. Like any loyal alumni, I was worried by this. So I called an old friend who keeps in touch, and asked:

"What's the matter with those kids?"

"Nothing, really," said my friend. "It's been a slow year because the guy who knew the four-letter words graduated. But we're after a junior college transfer for next year."

—*Comedy and Comment*

Graduate school: The place where a young scholar goes off his dad's payroll—and on to his wife's.

—Fletcher Knebel, *Detroit Free Press*

Graduate student: "Professor Socpsych, your study on the Harlem community structure was brutally profound and stimulating."

Professor: "Thank you. It is about to be published."

Graduate student: "Are conditions there really as bad as you described them?"

Professor: "Even more so! Depressing. Terribly depressing."

Graduate student: "Someone should do something about it."

Professor: "Yes, someone should do something about it. But, at least, now it is in the literature."

Graduate student: "What is your next project going to involve?"

Professor: "My next project? I am planning to test a few hypotheses dealing with non-involvement of educated groups of many talents in community affairs."

Graduate student: "That is interesting, but you will probably have some difficulty finding a subject group."

Professor: "That will be a problem."

Graduate student: "Well, I must be off. I am working on a paper that has a good chance to become part of the literature."

Professor: "Glad to see that you will soon be one of us."

—The Daily Illini, University of Illinois

Among all the student government campaign posters on the University of South Carolina campus walls was this wonderful little hand-printed message: "Draft Graduate Students—Care Enough to Send the Very Best."

—Bob Talbert,
Columbia State, Comedy and Comment

A reader concludes that the generation gap is the deep gully left in the bank account after sending a youngster to college.

—Clyde Moore,
Columbus Dispatch, Comedy and Comment

Three women were chatting at a bridge party, recounts Myron Scarbrough. One bragged that her college son had been awarded a fellowship. Another boasted that her college son had won an athletic trophy. And the third stated proudly that her college son had been granted amnesty.

—Bill Wildback, *Indianapolis News*

The college boy wrote home to his mother: "Mom, could you put an extra ten bucks in your next envelope to me? I need the money to buy a pair of pep pants to wear at our pep rally. They're supposed to put life into the party."

In her next letter to the boy, the mother put in two ten-dollar bills and a note: "Buy an extra pair for your dad and send them as quick as you can."

—Comedy and Comment

Guy down the street reports his son is graduating from college . . "and not a dollar too soon!"

—Mickey Porter, *Akron Beacon Journal*

CURRICULUM—COURSES—SUBJECTS

It was the grammar lesson, and the teacher was explaining the difference between a common and an abstract noun. "An example of a common noun is 'dog,' " she said, "for you can see a dog, but you cannot see anything that is in the abstract. For instance, have any of you ever seen 'abundance'?"

There was silence for a few moments. Then a little boy got up and said, "Please, ma'am, I have never seen a bun dance, but I have seen a cake walk."

—Sunshine Magazine

Booth tells, too, of the first year his father taught and at the end of the year a student in an English class practically floored him with this comment: "Mr. Booth, I want you to know how much you've done for me. If there's anything I know, it are English."

—Leo Aikman, Atlanta Constitution

On one of my book report forms I asked the following questions: "Is there a character in the book with whom you identify? If there is, who is it, and why do you identify with him?"

One of my bright but procrastinating eighth graders who was reporting on *The Odyssey* answered: "Polyphenus, because he was one-eyed, and I can't seem to see but one thing at a time."

—Arkansas Journal of Education

Professors of education are not the only ones who fail to set good examples. At our teacher placement day where administrators, candidates and professors mingle, I overheard this fragment of conversation: Student: "Is it true that low salaries have lowered the quality of teachers?" English professor: "Where'd you get that idea at?"

—Unknown

> He was a clever boy, but maladjusted.
> He wanted friends, but was mistrusted.
> In Latin class he was astute—
> Even the teacher thought him cute.
> His success became his ultimate delusion
> When he drew the asinine conclusion

That Latin should be required of all,
Since only here could he recall
The joys and affirmations
Of human warmth and conversations.
Little successes are dangerous things
When they create curriculum kings.

−Clifford E. Winkler, *Phi Delta Kappan*

The latest thing they're bringing home from the high school biology class is that you can't tell the sex of a chromosome unless you take off the genes and look.

−Jack Guinn, *Denver Post*

"I notice something very unusual in your work," he told the young lady. "Whenever you portray people, you paint them standing in a pool of water."

"Yes, sir," agreed the girl.

"Why is that?"

"Well, if you must know," she said, "I haven't learned how to paint feet."

−*Orlando Sentinel*

"New Math Spreads, Enlightening Kids but Mystifying Parents—Goal is to Introduce Advanced Concepts in Lowest Grades."—WGJ Headline.

To be outdone by a computer
Has always tied my mind in knots;
But now they've got one even cuter:
They're teaching calculus to tots!

−Tony Antolini

Everybody knows why congress voted against prayers in school: "Now that they have sex education, who knows what they'll be praying for?"

−*Comedy and Comment*

In Turkey, scientists are searching a mountain top for Noah's ark. In the West Indies they are probing the ocean floor for Columbus's flagship. This is the height of scientific endeavor in depth.

−Stephen Napierala,
Chicago Tribune, Comedy and Comment

Once upon a time, the animals decided they must do something heroic to meet the problems of a "new world." So they organized a school.

They adopted an activity curriculum consisting of running, climbing, swimming, and flying. To make it easier to administer the curriculum, all the animals took all the subjects.

The duck was excellent in swimming, in fact better than his instructor; but made only passing grades in flying and was very poor in running. Since he was slow in running, he had to stay after school and also drop swimming in order to practice running. This was kept up until his web feet were badly worn and he was only average in swimming. But average was acceptable in school, so nobody worried about that except the duck.

The rabbit started at the top of the class in running, but had a nervous breakdown because of so much make-up work in swimming.

The squirrel was excellent in climbing until he developed frustration in flying class where his teacher made him start from the ground up instead of from the treetop down. He also developed "charley horses" from overexertion and then got a C in climbing and a D in running.

The eagle was a problem child and was disciplined severely. In climbing class he beat all the others to the top of the tree, but insisted on using his own way of getting there.

At the end of the year, an abnormal eel that could swim exceedingly well, and also run, climb, and fly a little had the highest average and was valedictorian.

The prairie dogs stayed out of school and fought the tax levy because the administration would not add digging and burrowing to the curriculum. They apprenticed their child to a badger and later joined the groundhogs and gophers to start a successful private school.

—Dr. G.H. Reavis

A study by the American Council on Education involved asking freshman entering 61 colleges what careers they hope to follow. Here are some of the choices, precisely as written by the various students:

"Business," "Buseness," "Finance," "Holesail salisman," "Denestry," "Physist," "Technction," "Airnotics," "Treacher," "Stewardes," "Secteral," "Engenering."

One other was "undesided," while another was "Undecieded."
And these comments came from non-dropouts?

−Unknown

A fourth-grade teacher in Morgan, Minnesota, intercepted notes
passed between two boys. One wrote, "My shues srank." The
other replied, "You spellt shose rong."

−*Minneapolis Tribune, Comedy and Comment*

With all these sex education courses in school you'd think
there'd be no dropouts.

−Unknown

Mrs. Elaine Prude received into her second-grade class a young
man whose idea of sex education ran to rather specific words. She
was worrying aloud to her husband the other night about the new
vocabulary that her youngsters had acquired since the new student
arrived.

Her 13-year-old son Royce walked through the room and
listened a moment.

"I'll bet," he told his mother, "that you're the only second-
grade teacher in town whose Show and Tell has been rated X."

−Paul Crume, *Dallas Morning News*

Lew Shelke says the scientists have discovered so many substi-
tutes that it's hard to remember what was needed in the first
place.

−Bob Goddard, *St. Louis Globe-Democrat*

> My little boy is eight years old,
>   He goes to school each day;
> He doesn't mind the tasks they set—
>   They seem to him but play.
> He heads his class at raffia work,
>   And also takes the lead
> At making dinky paper boats—
>   But I wish that he could read.
> They teach him physiology,
>   And oh, it chills our hearts
> To hear our prattling innocent
>   Mix up his inward parts.
> He also learns astronomy
>   And names the stars by night;
> Of course he's very up-to-date,

But I wish that he could write.
They teach him things botanical,
　　They teach him how to draw.
He babbles of mythology
　　And gravitation's law;
The discoveries of science
　　With him are quite a fad.
They tell me he's a clever boy,
　　But I wish that he could add.

　　　　　　　　　　　　　　　　　—Peter McArthur

Speed reading is a necessity these days—or you will never get on the freeway.

　　　　　　　　　　　　　—*Spinnings* (San Mateo, Calif.)

We have a letter here from a man who complains that school children aren't taught proper penmanship these days. Pretty bitter about it, too. We'd print it only we can't make out the signature.

　　　　　　　　　　　　　　　　　　—Unknown

Neil V. Sullivan, superintendent of the Prince Edward County (Va.) Free Public School Association, which was established September, 1963, for Negro youngsters who had received no formal schooling since the Prince Edward County public schools were closed in 1959, tells this anecdote:

On the first day at one of our schools we had an assembly in the auditorium with a group of ten-year-olds who had never been to school. Our music teacher thought he should begin the assembly with "The Star Spangled Banner." He played the national anthem on the piano and then asked the youngsters to tell him the name of the song. No one seemed to have the slightest idea. Every face looked completely baffled until inspiration struck one small boy who had apparently been watching television all summer. "I know what it is," he said eagerly. "That's the baseball song."

　　　　　　　　　　　　　　　　　　NEA Journal

Some kids at Peabody High report that mini-skirts and mathematics sometimes don't mix. Teacher sent a gal to the blackboard to work out a problem, which took a lot of chalking and stretching. As the gal was reaching for the top of the blackboard, the lady teacher sighed, "Better sit down. That problem's too long for that short skirt."

　　　　　　　　　　　　　　　　　—*Comedy and Comment*

Clearing House has a proposal guaranteed to make every American schoolboy master mixed fractions within six weeks: to revise the rules of basketball so that a field goal counts 2 7/8, a free throw 1 1/5! Foul, says *Time Magazine.*

—Unknown

Hell has no fury, scorn or wrath
Like a tired parent tangling with modern math.

—Tommye Satterfield,
Memphis Commercial Appeal

When I came back to my home town last fall, I met a former mathematics teacher of mine. She was well in her 70's, and I didn't want her standing on the corner for a long time while we talked about old times. "Why don't you come over this evening to my folks' house and we'll have a nice long talk? We're on Grant Avenue. The number is 36144; have you got a pencil to write it down?" I asked.

"Oh, that won't be necessary," she replied. "It's three dozen and 12 squared."

—Mrs. Dean Binder, *Quote, Catholic Digest*

Brace yourself for some odd-sounding football if Congress decides to adopt the metric system next year. Imagine yourself at the Alabama-Mississippi game:

First and 9.144, with Alabama on the Mississippi 27.432 meter line. Avoirdupois takes the snap from Short-ton, fades, looks for a receiver, throws short to Troy. Troy is at the 13.716, at the 4.573, touchdown! Troy, the 1.8288 meter, 82.6480 kilogram end, has done it again! Alabama leads, 13 to 0."

Imagine explaining football to a woman under these circumstances.

—*Montgomery Journal*

Just as we thought! Lee Mann, writing in *Arithmetic Teacher* on. modern math: "Anyone with a forked tongue, two left thumbs, and a touch of insanity in the family will find it a natural."

—George Fuerman, *Houston Post*

A lady in Mountain Home, Idaho, recently wrote Editor Lloyd S. Waters of the weekly *News* asking how in the dickens people could teach their children good English when right on the front page of the *News* it said: "He had went on into town . . . ".

Forthright Editor Waters gave the only explanation he could think of:

"One of the proof readers hadn't come in yet and the other had just went out."

—Industrial Press Service, Quote

The teacher had taken her pupils for a trip through the Museum of Natural History.

"Well, Elmer," asked the father when the boy returned, "where did you go with your teacher this afternoon?"

"Huh," replied Elmer with disdain, "we went to a dead circus."

—Rotary Anchor (Alaska)

Look, Dick! Look, Jane! Mother and four children are at the airport. She is taking the children to Chicago for the weekend. She calls it an educational tour. Mother is crazy.

See Babs wave goodby? See Tad wave goodby? See Cissy wave goodby? See Stu pretend he is not with them. Stu is 13 years old.

See father? See father wave goodby? See father laugh? Why is father laughing so hard?

Now the family is going inside the big jet. See the stewardess? She is pretty. She is smiling. "Hello." she says. "Are you going to fly in the big airplane? Are you going to Chicago?"

"No," says Tad. "Isn't this the bus to Detroit?" Funny, funny Tad.

The stewardess helps the children find seats. She is still smiling. Why? Is she crazy?

The pretty stewardess shows the children how to fasten their seatbelts. She fastens Tad's for him. She pulls it so tight that he cannot talk. Isn't that funny?

The airplane zooms up into the air. Up, up, up. "Goodby, father," calls Babs. "Goodby, airport," calls Cissy. "Goodby, earth," calls Tad. "Good night, mother!" says Stu. "Can't you make them shut up?" What is mother saying? Oh, oh, we can't put that in the book.

The pretty stewardess brings the children little trays with a sandwich and something to drink. What is in the glass? A soft drink? Iced tea? Poison? See the stewardess trip over Tad's foot? See the drinks splash on her dress? Now we will never know what it was. See her step on the sandwiches? They were egg salad. She does not look so pretty any more.

The plane has landed in Chicago. The people on the plane say goodbye to the children. They are smiling. The stewardess is waving goodbye. She is smiling again. Why are they smiling? Because they are staying on the plane, that's why.

Did the children have fun on their educational tour? Will they have interesting things to tell about the trip when they return to school? What did the children see in Chicago?

They saw the rest rooms at the airport. They saw the rest rooms at Marshall Field's. They saw the rest rooms at the Adler Planetarium. And the rest rooms at the Museum of Science and Industry. And the rest rooms at the hotel.

What can mother tell? Where is mother? You saw her get on the plane for the return trip. Oh, oh. Maybe she is still locked in the rest room on the airplane.

—Betty Canary's Column,
Terre Haute Tribune-Star

A friend, learning Spanish from records, admits rather sheepishly he "went to sleep in class" the other day.

"But," he said, brightening up, "it wasn't wasted. I took a siesta instead of a nap."

—T.O. White, *Champaign-Urbana News-Gazette*

Anybody who thinks children have no originality should hear them spell.

—*Quote*

Grandpa says there was a start of sorts in sex education back in his country school days. His part was to furnish a little bird but the kid who was to bring the bees got stung so badly the whole thing was called off.

—Tom Eilerts, *Kansas City* (Mo.) *Times*

Message from Dr. Millicent McIntosh, president of Barnard College:

"There are several mispelled words in this report. They are not written by parints, kindergarten puples, enimy sergaents nor amature authors. They were taken from the examination papers of young men and women who have just had the benifit of one of the best things in life—a college education. Proper spelling is a sign of a well disaplined mind. In our opinnion, a graduate who can't write a definite precise analsis may turn out to be a type with a tendencie to split atoms that will assend us all through the cieling."

—Harold Helfer, *Laugh Book*

I frankly prefer the old dictionary, speaking not only as a teacher, but as a writer. Granted, language changes. But I don't see any great advantage in trying to hurry it along that way. They accept anything, because it is used.

"I don't know what would happen to the teaching of composition if you tried to follow that principal."

—Mark Schorer, quoted in *San Francisco Chronicle*

Noted authority up the country says many of the new science and mathematics curriculums being introduced are "puristic monsters." Lots of parents would agree with him completely if they knew what "puristic" means.

Memphis Commercial Appeal

A couple of Ramada guests were discussing the handwriting of their teen-age daughter, who had a bad habit of scrambling her letters. The father said: "Don't worry about it. If you're rich, you have a secretary. If you're poor, no one wants to hear from you anyway."

—Unknown

EDUCATION—EDUCATIONAL CRITICS

Education today is like the bottom half of a double boiler—it is boiling and bubbling busily but it doesn't really know what's cooking.

—John F. McCreary,
"Education of Health Personnel,"
Canadian Journal of Public Health, Quote

Education is something you get when your father sends you to college. But it isn't complete until you send your son there.

—Unknown

We often behave and plan as if the student's intellect exists in isolation from the rest of his being. We develop specialists who are reasonably capable of getting along in society, except when we ask them to improve society. We seldom teach students how or why they should integrate their special intellectual competencies with the rest of their experiences. Then we wonder why they are confused.

—Roland E. Barnes, "Steam Shovel on Campus,"
United Church Herald; Quote

Education replaces cocksure ignorance with thoughtful uncertainty.

—*Comedy and Comment*

It takes two to make a fight—one teacher and one classroom.

—*Comedy and Comment*

Former Vice President Hubert Humphrey has warned that while technology is playing an important and ever-increasing role in American life, it must not be allowed to become our master. He was defending the need for liberal arts education. A few more sonnets and a few less screwdrivers do seem to be needed in our gimmick-happy society.

—*Atlanta* (Ga.) *Journal, Quote*

How to Become an Instant Critic of Education

1. *Give yourself a title.* Almost any title will do as long as it does not imply that you have a responsible position in public education. Military titles are among the best.

2. *Find some fault with the public schools.* This is rather easy in an enterprise involving 35 million Americans. It is best not to visit the schools. This may produce conflicting evidence and cramp your style.

3. *Avoid the study of research in education.* The single instance is much more effective as a device for making your point; besides, research findings will often destroy your argument.

4. *Do not mention education's conflicting goals.* Your own private ideal of the good life must be the only true goal of education. After all, what is good for you is good for the country.

5. *Blame all school weaknesses on a single cause.* Multiple causation is likely to be uninteresting and hard for the public to understand. The "devil theory" is by far the most popular and effective. John Dewey makes a good devil; dig him up and hang him every five years, or an anonymous group like professional educators, school administrators, or educationists.

6. *Never advocate a positive program.* If pressed, you can refer modestly to sub-selected aspects of your own education. European education is also a good model if your audience is not familiar with it.

7. *Distinguish between "our" children and "other" people's children.* With "our" children, stress the need for sympathy, understanding, and a program for individual differences. With "other people's" children, stress discipline and hard work.

8. *Choose terms for their emotional appeal.* For example, "discipline" is a good word but "social adjustment" is bad.

9. *Write primarily for the popular press.* Not only do you gain a wider following but, more importantly, you will also not have to be so careful with what you write.

10. *Cash in your new role as an expert.* Any book you write is bound to be a best seller. This will lead to lectures, television appearances, and other roads to fame and fortune.

                              —E.Graham Pogue, Curriculum Bulletin,
                                  University of Oregon, September, 1969

"Disenchanted Teachers—tell me your gripes. Am collecting material for book on schools."

                                                —Classified ad,
                                  Saturday Review, Phi Delta Kappan

Have you heard about the new aptitude test for classifying prospective and new educators? It's called the "elephant test." Here's how it works:

The candidate group is blindfolded and an elephant is brought in for them to investigate. If a candidate feels and concentrates on the tusk, he is urged to become a football coach. The tusk is spear-like which suggests the combative idea and thus aggressiveness. The candidate who seizes the elephant's trunk is steered into budget, curriculum or PTA work since the trunk is snake-like, which suggests hissing.

When another candidate feels the large ear and describes the elephant thusly, he is urged to become a heat reducer and cooler-offer such as an executive assistant. The elephant's ear, you see, is used as a fan.

If a candidate grasps the elephant's sturdy leg and describes the animal as tree-like it is recommended that he become a principal, for a principal is always up a tree or out on a limb.

How to Run Away from an Educational Program

Most educational discussions become, sooner or later, a desperate attempt to escape from the problem. This is often done clumsily, causing unnecessary embarrassment and leaving the group without the comfortable feeling of having disposed of the problem. A "cultural lag" is evident in this situation. Educational leaders have long since worked out an adequate battery of techniques for dodging the issue.

In the course of a misspent youth[1] the writer and his friends have sat at the feet of many eminent practitioners of this art and have compiled a list of their devices. The list, of course, is only tentative, partial, incomplete, a mere beginning, etc., but it should at least give group leaders a command of alternative modes of retreat, enabling them to withdraw their forces gracefully and to leave the problem baffled and helpless. In the interest of promoting the Christian spirit, we must dispense with acknowledging the sources of the following items:

1. Find a scape-goat and ride him. Teachers can always blame administrators, administrators can blame teachers, both can blame parents, and everyone can blame the social order.
2. Profess not to have *the* answer. This lets you out of having any answer.
3. Say that we must not move too rapidly. This avoids the necessity of getting started.
4. For every proposal set up an opposite and conclude that the "middle ground" (no motion whatever) represents the wisest course of action.
5. Point out that any attempt to reach a conclusion is only a futile "quest for certainty." Doubt and indecision "promote growth."
6. When in a tight place, say something which the group cannot understand.

---

[1]Much of the misspent youth to which the author refers was squandered at PEA workshops, as a curriculum consultant with the Eight-Year Study, and on PEA's Evaluation staff.

7. Look slightly embarrassed when the problem is brought up. Hint that it is in bad taste, or too elementary for mature consideration, or that any discussion of it is likely to be misinterpreted by outsiders.

8. Say that the problem "cannot be separated" from other problems; therefore no problem can be solved until all other problems have been solved.

9. Carry the problem into other fields; show that it exists everywhere, hence is of no concern.

10. Point out that those who see the problem do so by virtue of personality traits; e.g., they are unhappy and transfer their dissatisfaction to the area under discussion.

11. Ask what is meant by the question. When it is clarified, there will be no time left for the answer.

12. Discover that there are all sorts of "dangers" in any specific formulation of conclusions: dangers of exceeding authority or seeming to, of asserting more than is definitely known, of misinterpretation, misuse by uninformed teachers, criticism (and of course the danger of revealing that no one has a sound couclusion to offer).

—Paul B. Diederich

Adult education is a strenuous effort to learn about things that bored you when you were still young enough to profit from them.

—Burton Hillis, *Better Homes and Gardens*

How about all those job changes in Washington? A reporter asked Robert Finch how he had fared as Secretary of Health, Education and Welfare and Finch said: "My education grew—but my health and welfare languished."

—*Current Comedy*

The Free Activity class was in session—everyone *must do as he pleases,* whether he wants to or not. A new pupil, unaccustomed to this procedure, comes in. He wanders about in confusion. Soon a lad more sympathetic and understanding than the rest nudges him and whispers: "You better find an outlet or you'll catch it from the teacher."

—Eugene Bertin, *Senior Citizen*

Why have a department of Health, Education and Welfare? Well, after you pay for the first two, you'll need somewhere to turn.

—*Changing Times*

—————————————————ELEMENTARY SCHOOL—————————————————

The teacher described vividly the misery in the mountain valley brought on by the flood and the cold. The fourth-grade class decided to send a box of edibles and wearables in relief. The young ones were a little tardy in bringing in the donations.

The fourth grader assigned to write the note of transmittal came up with this: "We're sorry we're late sending you these things and we hope the suffering is not over."

—Leo Aikman, *Comedy and Comment*

In the same community a youngster asked his teacher at Bedford Elementary School the name of the man whose statue adorns the main corridor.

"That's the man who founded this school," the teacher told him. "The school is named after him."

The boy thought a moment and said: "Oh—Mr. Elementary?"

—Unknown

A third-grade teacher began a discussion of Brotherhood Week in this way: "Does any one know what week this is? Well, it's a very special week when we all try to understand each other better, and to learn to live together in peace and harmony. This is especially important in cities, where there are so many of us and we all live so closely together. Now does this give any of you a clue? Can anybody tell me the name of this special week?" A period of contemplation followed, after which a girl in the class raised her hand. She volunteered: "Is it Child Prevention Week?"

—Robert McMorris, *Omaha World-Herald*

Visiting the third-grade room, the school supervisor was amazed at the ready and accurate history answers given by Jimmy, an eight-year-old pupil, and asked, "Jimmy, where do you find out about history?"

"I look in my schoolbooks or reference books," he said, "and if it isn't there I ask grandma."

—Greg Williams

A grade school teacher, in trying to get over the concept of distance, asked her pupils whether they lived close or far away from the school. She got a number of answers, but the one she liked best was the young moppet who told her, "I think I live pretty close. Every time I come home, my mother says, 'Good grief, are you home already?' "

—*Sparta* (Wisconsin) *Herald, Quote*

From the Mouths of Babes. From the Mt. Carmel, Illinois, *Republican-Register:* "The fifth-grade chorus sang, 'Nobody Knows the Trouble I've Been.' "

Scholastic Teacher

In a elementary school the other day, a fifth grader was caught reading a "girlie magazine" (with lurid pictures) and the teacher marched him to the office for a talk with the principal. The principal was up to his job. Gave the moppet a severe talking to. "And now," he commanded, "you sit down right now and write a letter to your mother, telling what you've done." The kid sat down, started his letter: "Dear Mother: This morning I took daddy's magazine to school . . ."

—Emmett Watson, *Comedy and Comment*

A fifth-grade teacher asked Johnny, "Who signed the Declaration of Independence?" Johnny thought a moment and shot back, "I don't know who signed the damned thing!" "What did you say?" asked the surprised teacher. "I said I don't know who signed the damned thing," repeated Johnny.

At the close of the class period the teacher called the boy's father and said, "You'll have to come down to school—I have a problem with Johnny." Next day the indignant father came and was told about Johnny's shocking answer. "Well, he said to the teacher, let me take the lad into the hall and talk this over." They went out and he began. "Now son, it's true that we live across the tracks but at least we can be honest and truthful. Now son, if you signed that damned thing, admit it!"

—Unknown

EXAMINATIONS

The story is told of the famed Professor Eliot of Harvard. The students in his class were asked to sign a statement when they took their examination that they had received no help in answering the questions.

One of the bright lads approached the professor's desk and said with a straight face: "I can't sign that statement, sir. While I was working on the exam, I frequently asked God for help."

Dr. Eliot let his glance run over the boy's examination paper. Then, also with a straight face, he said: "Go ahead and sign it, son. You didn't receive any help."

—Liguorian, Quote

Sixth-Grade Slip-ups

Describe the circulation of the blood. *Answer:* It flows down one leg and up the other.

The spinal column is a long bunch of bones. The head sits on top and you sit on the bottom.

To prevent head cold, use an agonizer to spray nose until it drops into your throat.

Why do we not raise silk worms in the U. S.? *Answer:* We get our silk from rayon. He is a larger animal and gives more silk.

A dinosaur became extinct after the flood because they were too big to get into the ark.

One by-product of cattle raising is calves.

How do bacteria reproduce? They multiply and then divide.

In the spring the salmon ascends fresh water to spoon.

What kind of a noun is trousers? *Answer:* an uncommon noun because it is singular at the top and plural at the bottom.

—Colorado School Journal

Backward, turn backward, o time, in your flight, and tell me just one thing I studied last night!

—Sunshine Magazine

Alibi-ography for Students

What to say—
When you are given an objective test:
  "It doesn't let you express yourself."
When you are given an essay test:
  "It's so vague. You don't know what's expected."
When you are given many minor tests:
  "Why not have a few big ones. This keeps you on the edge all the time."

When you are given a few major tests:
    "Too much depends on each one."
When you are given no tests:
    "It's not fair. How can he possibly judge what we know?"
When every part of the subject is taken up in class:
    "Oh, he just follows the book."
When you are asked to study a part of the subject by yourself:
    "Why, we never even discussed it!"
When the course is in lecture form:
    "We never get a chance to say anything."
When the course consists of informal lecture and discussion:
    "He just sits there. Who wants to hear the students? They
    don't know how to teach the course."
When detailed material is presented:
    "What's the use? You forget it all after the exam anyway."
When general principles are presented?
    "What did we learn? We knew all that before we took the
    course."

                                    —Robert Tyson, Curriculum Bulletin,
                                    University of Oregon, September, 1969

    At Sir George, students taking an examination in philosophy
were asked to answer the one-word question: "Why?"
    One student's reply: "Why not?"
    He was awarded an A.

                                    —Bruce Taylor, *Montreal Star*

    The first grader was taking a simple test. One item showed two
drawings, one of a man chopping wood, the other of a man
reading a book. She was required to circle the picture that showed
"a man at work." She circled the reader and was marked wrong.
And that, says John Esty, Jr., headmaster of Taft School in
Connecticut, shows what's wrong with tests. What the teacher
didn't know was that the child's father was a college professor,
who read books at work and chopped wood for fun.

                                    —*Changing Times*

From Examination Papers

    —Tennyson wrote "In Memorandum."
    —Louis XVI was gelatined during the French Revolution.

—Gravitation is that which if there were none we should all fly away.

—Algebraic symbols are used when you do not know what you are talking about.

—Queen Elizabeth was tall and thin, but she was a stout Protestant.

—An Equinox is a man who lives near the north pole.

—The five great powers of Europe are water power, steam power, electricity, horses, and camels.

—The battle of Cowpens was a battle fought in the stockyards during the Civil War.

—Unknown

About this time of the year, teachers everywhere start coming up with the howlers they got on exams during the session. They make interesting reading.

"Strategy," wrote a student on one of the lists furnished us, "is when you don't let the enemy know you are out of ammunition, but keep on firing."

"A virgin forest," defined another, "is a forest in which the hand of man has never set foot."

—Paul Crume, *Dallas Morning News*

A student wrote on an examination paper just before the Christmas holidays, "Only the Lord knows the answer to this question. Merry Christmas."

When he got his paper back, the prof had written: "The Lord gets an A; you get an F. Happy New Year."

—Barnes-Ross Co., *Nuggets, Quote*

School Examination Boners.

—The equator is a menagerie lion running around the earth.

—To keep in good health, inhale and exhale once a day and gymlastics.

—The sacred chickens of the Romans were the Vestal Virgins.

—Esau wrote fables and sold his copyright for a mess of potash.

—Average is a next. Hens lay on the average.

—The epistles were the wives of the apostles.

—To germinate is becoming a naturalized German.

—Invoice: Anglo-Saxon for the conscience.

—A mayor is a female horse.

—An optimist is a doctor who looks after the eyes. A pessimist looks after the feet.

—A papul bull was a ferocious bull kept by the Popes to trample on protestants.

—A Protestant is a wicked woman who gets her living by living an immortal life.

—The dome of the Sistine Madonna was painted by Michael Angelo.

—Laugh Book

A Kirkwood, Missouri, teacher found this gem in a geography test paper: "I think our state is the most beautiful in the whole country. Of course, I may be a little pregnant."

—Quote

Here are a few educational "boners" made by 11-year-old English children in recent tests, which have just been published in London:

A crisis is a thing which hangs up in the winter and comes down in the summer as a butterfly.

An active verb shows action, as "He kissed her," and a passive verb shows passion, as "She kissed him."

A republic is a country where no one can do anything in private.

Bookkeeping is the art of not returning books borrowed.

Contralto is a low sort of music that only ladies can sing.

Amen means "That's the lot."

—Sunshine Magazine

Question on an examination paper in the English class: "What is poetic license?"

Answer from star pupil: "A poetic license is a license you get from the post office to keep poets. You get one also if you want to keep a dog. It costs $4 and you call it a dog license."

—American Opinion, Quote

——————————— HOLIDAYS AND SEASONAL———————————

Youngsters starting school are receiving dental care instructions: See dentist at regular intervals; brush teeth after every meal.

And watch out for shovers at drinking fountains.

—Lou Erickson,
Atlanta Journal, Comedy and Comment

The opening of school always brings forth a number of amusing incidents, and one of the best is that reported by a teacher in the tenement district who was trying to impress her young pupils with the importance of being original.

She illustrated by saying: "Mickey, repeat these sentences in your own words: 'I see a cow. The cow is pretty. The cow can run.' "

Mickey said: "Boy, lamp de cow. Ain't she a honey! An' I ask you, kin she take it on th' lam!"

—*Sunshine Magazine*

> Toes get snubbed, there's a skinned-up shin,
> Never mind, mom, all these will mend.
> Over the hill and 'round the bend,
> With shirt tail flying in the wind,
> Betcha he'll be the first one in
> The swimming hole—school's out again.
>
> —Bee Bacherig, *Memphis Commercial Appeal*

George Jay reports about his small nephew who wrote a letter to Santa Claus telling him he wanted his bicycle fixed and his violin broken.

—Bill Kennedy, *Los Angeles Herald Examiner*

In Detroit Mark Beltaire told about the seven-year-old daughter of a teacher who was supposed to draw the Nativity scene for the class. She did a fine job, complete with Jesus, Mary, Joseph, and all the scenery. But in one corner was a short, fat man who didn't jibe with the original. Asked to explain him, the girl answered: "That's Round John Virgin."

—Unknown

December is whistle blowing on Friday night up at the schools and the passing of a basketball; it is a salt-crusted roast—pink inside—served with horseradish sauce; it is a string of mallards and blacks beating downwind before a curtain of snow; it is galoshes; and wrapping packages; and wood in the fireplace, and the family gathered around the tree on Christmas Eve.

—Unknown

———————————————— HOMEWORK————————————————

A very much discouraged teacher examining a boy's homework turned to him and said, "I don't see how one person could make so many mistakes."

"It wasn't just one person," said the youngster. "It was four—me, mom, pop and Aunt Mary."

—Nuggets, Barnes-Ross Co., *Quote*

Apparently it's some sort of unwritten rule that a well-stocked home library includes every kind of book except the one that a high school child needs at the last moment for a term paper.

—Quote

The first week of school is fraught, if that's the right word, with crises.

One night, after dinner, a small boy, just old enough to fill out those enrollment cards, walked into the kitchen and asked his mother: "What's sex?"

She had been expecting that sort of question and, true to the child guidance books, had an answer prepared, just in case.

She sighed, dried her hands on her apron and said, "Let's go back to your room."

He sat at his desk, where he had been working. She sat on the bed.

And she delivered the lecture.

Some ten minutes later, the lecture done, she asked: "Now, do you have any questions?"

"Yeah," said her son, picking up his enrollment card, "How'm I gonna get all that stuff in this one little bitty square?"

—George Dolan,
Ft. Worth Star Telegram, Comedy and Comment

My husband was absorbed in his favorite TV program when our young son ventured to ask him about a homework problem. "Dad," he said, "where are the Alps?"

"Ask your mother," came the reply. "She puts everything away."

—Mrs. V.T., *Woman*

The Max Anderson's 11-year-old, Kirk, who's a fifth grader, looked up from his homework one evening, sighed and mentioned:

"The trouble with current events is that they keep happening every day."

—Comedy and Comment,
George Dolan, *Ft. Worth Star Telegram*

Many are the times I've yearned to learn again the things I learned so super-superficially—history, French, geometry—things I gave a grudging eye back in dear old Public High.

Could I but study now, I've said, I'd get to work and stuff my head; my brain would soak up facts like a blotter; I'd burn the midnight hundredwatter.

Well, now some unexpected help has come from little George (the whelp!); I've got my opportunity—he brings his homework all to me.

—Scott Corbett

Small fry to friend outside his teenage sister's bedroom: "It's called homework. They scatter some books around and then talk about boys."

—The National Future Farmer

JUNIOR–SENIOR HIGH SCHOOL

A high school dropout is frequently a chap who is face to face with the necessity of going to work to support his automobile.

—Unknown

The boy whose father used to drop him off at school, and then drive on to work, now has a son who drops him off at work and then drives on to school.

—Lowell Nussbaum

The ninth-grade pupil, carried away with his own rhetoric in the story of the launching of a carrier, wound up his theme: "Miss Smith smashed a bottle of champagne against the bow of the USS Missouri with unerring aim, and then while the huge crowd cheered madly, she slid majestically down the greasy ways into the sea."

—Unknown

If you're wondering who buys the cars rolling off Detroit assembly lines, California may have the answer. Recently, a report to the state board of education disclosed that a high school for 2,000 students usually requires a parking lot six acres in size.

—Christian Science Monitor

Myron Scarbrough reports that a high school freshman he knows says her home is organized like Congress. Her mother is Speaker of the House and her father is the whip.

—Laugh Book

Student note to one of the officials at a high school: "In protest for a rough ride to school, I am burning my bus card."

—Emmett Watson, *Seattle Post, Intelligencer*

The high school teacher asked the senior class to stand up one at a time and state their ambition in life. Finally it was Jane's turn.

"I would like to reverse the theory of evolution," she said.

Teacher: "Please explain."

Jane: "I want to make monkeys out of men."

—David Wilkening,
Orlando Sentinel, Comedy and Comment

The seventh-grade class was holding a magazine-subscription sale. The morning after the sale started one boy reported that he had already sold $20 worth.

"How did you manage to sell so many so quickly?" he was asked.

"I sold them all to one family," the boy replied. "Their dog bit me!"

—Charlie Wadsworth,
Orlando Sentinel, Comedy and Comment

A high school student was filling out an application for after-school employment at a store. As he pondered over some of the questions, the personnel manager came up to help. The first thing that caught his eye was the space marked: "Salary desired?"

Next to it was written: "Yes."

—Sunshine Magazine

Many teachers and former teachers have written books about their school experiences. Recently a group of eighth-grade pupils at Public School 52 in Buffalo, New York, wrote a book with the encouragement of their teacher, Teresa Lopata. Titled "Miseries United," the 5¢ paperback has proven to be a best-seller in and around the school. According to the youngsters:

"School is dropping all your books in the hall when you have a miniskirt on."

"School is being told to keep your love life out of school, and you don't even have a love life."

"School is when you have to go to the lavatory and the teacher doesn't believe you."

"School is hearing the fire-alarm bell when you are in the gym, and you're only half dressed."

"School is having all the right answers but one, the one you're asked."

—Unknown

"Now, Arthur," a teacher asked a member of her class, "can you point out to us some evidences that we really have religious liberty in this country?"

"Well, for one thing," replied the high school student, "anybody can join any church he wishes, and then attend the Sunday services as seldom as he wants to, and still remain on the roll—if he just pays his dues."

—Roy A. Brenner, *Laugh Book*

──────────── NON–TEACHING STAFF ────────────

In the educational world a school administrator knows something about everything, a specialist knows everything about something—and the custodian knows everything.

—*Contemporary Education*

A consultant is a well-paid expert brought in at the last minute to share the blame.

—*Milpitas* (Calif.) *Post*

Mr. John P. Jones, Supt.

Dear Mr. Jones:

In answer to your ad in this morning's paper seeking a new secretary, I would like to be interviewed for the position. My background includes a college education, two years of business school, and I type a good 50 words a minute.

Very sincerely,
Ethel Smith

Miss Ethel Smith
215 Main Street
Milford, Texas

Dear Miss Smith:

Thank you for your letter of June 10th. I am sorry to inform you that we are looking for a secretary with more experience. The job also requires someone capable of typing at a rate of 75 words or more per minute.

Very truly yours,
John B. Jones

Mr. John B. Jones
Jones Production Company
67 Tenth Avenue
Milford, Texas

Dear Mr. Jones:

I read your ad in the paper this morning and I would like to take the job because I'm short of money. I don't know how to type and I would have to have Wednesdays off because that's the day I do my modeling jobs if my agency should call me. I would have to leave the job at four-thirty each day because that would give me just time enough to get home and eat and catch another bus for my seven o'clock theatre workshop. My salary also would have to be at least a hundred dollars a week because I would be wasting my time with anything under that. I am enclosing a photo of myself in a bikini bathing suit that won me the title of "Miss White Wall Tires of 1963."

Very sincerely,
Fifi Duncan

Miss Fifi Duncan
410 Rampart Street
Milford, Texas

Dear Miss Duncan:

When can you report for work? We've tried to locate you by

phone and wire. When you receive this please phone this office and I shall arrange to pick you up in my own car.

Very truly yours,
John B. Jones

—Unknown

Drumright, Oklahoma's, Gerry Jones borrows a word or two from Edgar Allen Poe to voice the plaint of many an office slave. ... She titles it "A Secretary's Dream."

> Once upon a noonday dreary
> Sat Miss Steno, weak and weary,
> Dreaming of the day unknown when
> She could clobber Mr. Drone, then
> Turn upon her heel and, chin high,
> Sniff at Mr. Drone and spin by
> Through the halls and to the stairwell,
> Bidding one and all her farewell,
> To be seen (like Lost Lenore
> And the Raven)—Nevermore.

—Roger Devlin

A gorgeous blonde was applying for an office position. She had all the lines and curves of a satisfactory steno. She also had good recommendations, though the office manager was less interested in them than in her.

"You have impressed me very favorably, Miss Smith," he said. "And I believe you will like being here if you are interested in this splendid opportunity for advances."

—Unknown

The Modern Model Secretary

> When I was a lass, I served a term
>   As an office girl in a school game firm,
> I washed the windows and swept the floor
>   And I cranked that Ditto—like I never did before.
> Oh!! cranked that Ditto so carefully
>   That now I am a model sec-re-tree!

Oh! I typed all the letters and I filed all the
    trash
I licked all the stamps and I counted all
    the cash.
I nursed all the students and fed them
    rations,
And answered all the phones and never
    lost my patience.
Oh! I answered all the phones so patiently,
      That I soon became the model sec-re-tree.
Oh I rang all the bells and I even took
    attendance
I listened to dictation and corrected every
    sentence.
I filed all those cards and never made a
    sound,
And I even made a profit on the damn
    lost and found.
Oh I handled all those things so efficiently
      That I soon became a model sec-re-tree.
I never had a date and I devoted all my
    time
To making three copies of every student's
    crime.
I pleased all trustees and regents few
      And salesman and mailman and janitors too!
Oh I soothed all these men so courteously
      I soon earned my title as a sec-re-tree.
I listened to the profs and endured all their
    grumbles,
I counted all the books and never made a
    rumble.
I prepared all reports and never once was
    late.
I brewed all the liquors for the coffee
    break.
I brewed all those liquors so faithfully
      That I soon became the model sec-re-tree.
Now heed my advice girls—you're not just
    a fool—

You are the only people who can run a
school!

Michigan Elementary Principal

The Secretary's Day

A.M.

"He hasn't come in yet."
"I expect him in any minute."
"He just sent word he'd be a little late."
"He's been in, but he went out again."
"He's gone to lunch."

P.M.

"I expect him in any minute."
"He hasn't come back yet. Can I take a message?"
"He's somewhere in the building. His hat is here."
"Yes, he was in, but he went out again."
"I don't know whether he'll be back or not."
"No, he's gone for the day."

Bank Notes

Two secretaries were discussing their problems over a cup of coffee. One of them said, "All I asked the boss was, 'Do you want the carbon copy double spaced too?'"

−*The Garber Rotarian,* Garber, Oklahoma

A principal was giving his periodic lecture on efficiency. He emphatically declared that the home, including four children under five and a dog, could and should be run like an office.

"You must do things as they come up, that's the secret. Never put off anything or it starts to pile up. Do things at once. The minute something crosses my desk, I immediately" . . . [pause, then he added sheepishly,] "give it to my secretary to do."

−Unknown

"Did I hear you correctly?" asked the new secretary. "Make 26 copies of every letter?"

"That's right," answered the boss, "please do."

"May I ask why?"

"We file one under each letter of the alphabet, then we are sure of finding them," replied the harried man.

−Unknown

Did you hear about the two bulls pastured just across the fence from a whole herd of lovely heifers. Each day the bulls would jump the fence for social visits and it was a happy arrangement for all.

Then one day the older bull didn't quite clear the top wire; suffering grievous injuries, he cried out bitterly against the fates. "Look at it this way," said the other one, trying to be a comfort, "now you can be a consultant."

—Unknown

An ironworker was nonchalantly sitting on the beams atop a new skyscraper as the pneumatic hammers made a nerve-jangling racket and the compressor below shook the whole structure. When he came down, a sidewalk superintendent stopped him and remarked, "I'm amazed at your calmness up there. How did you happen to have the courage to get into this kind of work?"

"Well," explained the ironworker, "I used to drive a school bus but my nerves gave out."

—Unknown

The man who gets into a cage with a dozen lions impresses everyone but a school bus driver.

—Doug Larson, Door County (Wis.) *Advocate*

The father of a seven-year-old boy, curious regarding his son's grasp of the economics of education, asked the lad: "Do you know who owns the school you go to?"

The little boy replied without a moment's hesitation: "Yes—the janitor."

Surprised, but also intrigued, the father asked a number of his son's friends the same question . . . and found that none of them were in doubt about it; the janitor owned the school building.

—John D. McAulay, "The Elementary Principal:
Anachronism or What?" *Education Age*

──────────── NURSERY SCHOOL—KINDERGARTEN ────────────

The service or services to meet our needs do not exist, and we have a blank area which I hope will soon be filled. The situation is a little like the story of the kindergarten teacher who in desperation asked her class to paint whatever they saw outside the window. All but Johnny did the routine job. But Johnny cautiously painted sky one third of the way down from the top of his paper, and earth and trees one third of the way up from the bottom of his paper, leaving the middle third absolutely blank. The teacher said to him, "But Johnny, look out there at the horizon. Don't you see that the earth and the sky meet?" To which Johnny replied, "Yeah. But I've been there. And they don't."

—Unknown

It was the end of the term at the progressive nursery school, and a mother was waiting downstairs to see the principal about registering her child for the next term. When the clock struck three, a horde of children raced out, practically throwing the visitor over. The last child, instead of running off with the others, stopped and apologized. At that moment the principal appeared.

"Please excuse that youngster," he pleaded, pointing to the little gentleman who was leaving the building in an orderly manner. "He's a new pupil and he isn't adjusted to us yet."

—Unknown

In our parish school in Chicago, the kindergarten children were working diligently on an assignment; they were each to draw a picture of Colonel Glenn's orbits around the world.

The first girl to finish brought her picture up to Sister for an appraisal.

"Lovely, lovely," Sister said, "but who is this lady down in the corner?"

"Oh, I thought you'd know," said the little girl. "That's Kate Canaveral."

—Sister Mary Philip, *Catholic Digest, Quote*

A pre-schooler with considerable TV watching experience wasn't stumped for a remedy when her mother lost her voice because of laryngitis. "You got no sound, mama," diagnosed the tot. "Maybe you need a new tube."

—Kelly Fordyce's *Sunday Smiles*

The dangers of show-and tell remain with us even when our children are out of school for the summer.

A small lad arrived at kindergarten the other day and proudly informed his teacher that his daddy had fallen off the stepladder while he was painting the kitchen.

"Was he badly hurt?" asked the teacher, appropriately horrified.

"No'm," the boy assured her. "Didn't even spill his beer."

—Lydel Sims, *Laugh Book*

Susie's mother was pleased that the nursery school was working on courtesy and good manners. Every day Susie would come home and tell her what she'd learned that day. One day Susie came home and announced proudly, "When you're seduced, you always shake hands."

—*Mississippi Educational Advance,*
The Education Digest

A kindergarten teacher gave each pupil a chunk of soap and said: "Carve whatever you like."

After a bit, she circulated among them, asking what each boy and girl was making.

The answers went like this:

"A Gun."

"A Duck."

"A Face."

"A Boat."

"Soap Flakes."

—George Dolan,
Ft. Worth Star-Telegram, Comedy and Comment

I am told that a kindergarten pupil came home the other day and was asked the inevitable question by his mother: "What did you learn in school today?"

"I learned," he said, "that four and four makes nine."

"But that's wrong," said his mother.

"Well," said the kid, "in that case, I didn't learn anything."

—James Dent,
Charleston Gazette, Comedy and Comment

A kindergarten youngster said he was born in a drive-in theater. His parents had stopped there to ask directions to the maternity hospital—and they got interested in the picture.

—Earl Wilson, *Quote*

The teacher was explaining to the first-day kindergarten pupils:

"And if anyone wants to go to the washroom, hold up two fingers."

From the back of the room came a soft question: "How's that gonna help?"

— *Santa Fe Magazine*

A third-grade pupil had a talk with his little brother, who was getting ready to enroll in kindergarten.

"Remember," he warned, "in school when the teacher says 'no,' she means it. It's not like around home!"

—*Christian Science Monitor,* quoted in
Minneapolis Tribune

Ever have trouble describing how you feel with flu? Then listen to a quick summary by a scholar in Mrs. John Hooser's kindergarten class at First Methodist Church at Clarksdale, Mississippi:

"I feel like I've got ice cream on the brain."

—Lydel Sims, *Memphis Commercial Appeal*

PARENTS

The teacher sent a note home with Johnny asking his mother to see that he had a bath. The next day Johnny handed the teacher this note:

"Der Miss Smith. Johnny comes to school to git learnt, not smelt. He ain't no rose."

—*Duke Power Magazine, Quote*

"Thank you kindly for your letter regarding Johnny's lack of progress in school. Your suggestion for a conference is most interesting. We live on Shortshrift Street on the shore of Park Lake and cordially invite you to drop in at your earliest convenience."

—"Chalk Dust," *Nations Schools.* Used with permission.

After the first two or three days of having the youngsters out of school, mothers begin to wonder why no one has gotten around to putting tranquilizers in chewing gum.

—Clyde Moore, *Columbus Dispatch*

Most concerned fathers want their girls to attend sex-education classes in school. And they want them to go out with boys and enjoy drive-in movies, hayrides, and beach parties. They only ask that they wait until they're old enough. Say about 35.

—Unknown

"What did your father say about wrecking the car?"
"Shall I omit the bad words?"
"Certainly."
"He didn't say anything."

—*Comedy and Comment*

Parents of teen-agers claim their hardest job is getting their kids to realize that "no" can be a complete sentence.

—Mickey Porter,
Akron Beacon Journal, Comedy and Comment

Today's accent may be on youth, but the stress is on parents.

—*Sparks* (Ga.) *Eagle*

There is undue stress on early sophistication, says a parenthood bulletin. Next: Contraceptive bubble gum.

—Lou Erickson, *Atlanta Journal*

Even yet, the standard of living isn't nearly high enough. For example, there are still parents who own only one car and their unfortunate children have to walk as much as four or five blocks to school.

—Olin Miller, *Thomaston* (Ga.) *Times*

Who taught me all my ABC's, and P's and Q's, too,
If you please? You did.
Who stopped the tantrums that I threw, and taught me
How to tie a shoe? You did.
Who taught me all about fair play, and what kids should
And shouldn't say, you did!
Who sewed the buttons on my clothes,
And taught me not to pick my nose? You did!
Who got fed up with parent's work,
Slaving daily like a turk, with less pay than a soda jerk,
And quit to find some other work? You did.

—*Mad*

An Edina man writes that a German visitor was guest of honor at his house recently during a party. When a housewife asked the guest what he noticed first about Americans the man replied, "The remarkable way parents obey their children."

—*Comedy and Comment*

It seems no matter how you encourage your children to tread the path of righteousness, they insist on following in your footsteps.

—Mickey Porter,
Akron Beacon Journal, Comedy and Comment

A University of Wisconsin sociologist has come to this conclusion: "Man is no longer king in his castle. There has been a palace revolution and the father has emerged as the court jester."

—Journal of Insurance, Quote

While Elsie Kennedy was art supervisor for Clark County, Kentucky, schools, she recalls a letter a mother sent to a fourth-grade teacher.

"Dear Mrs. Howard," the letter read, "If you will excuse my son to go to the bathroom at 3 p.m. each day the bus ride home will be more pleasant for all concerned."

—Comedy and Comment

Frazzled baby-sitter to returning parents: "Don't apologize. I wouldn't be in any hurry to come home either."

—Unknown

The smile of the child, as he starts for school,
Is a bit restrained, as a general rule.
The teacher's smile, in the same way, tends
To droop a bit as vacation ends.
But the smile much wider than the others—
As the summer riot ends—is Mother's.

—Bradley L. Morrison, *Minneapolis Tribune*

The bill came for straightening junior's teeth. Now dad needs braces.

—Unknown

———————————— PRIMARY GRADES ————————————

Ricky Renner, six, a first grader, came home the other day to announce: "I'm having trouble with my consulates and bowels." Isn't everybody?

—Troy Gordon, *Tulsa World*

Teacher was asking first graders to tell briefly "the lesson" they saw in different children's stories. "Goldilocks and the Three Bears" stumped them all until little Johnny raised his hand and shouted: "Keep your cotton pickin' fingers out of my porridge."

—Unknown

Two first graders watched a sleek foreign sports car whiz past. "Boy," one exclaimed, "that's the 1965 jet-carburetor job with the independent nylon suspension system!"

"Oh, no," the second boy said. "That's the counter-weighted 50-liter job with torsion bar, model number CG 221—and three other numbers we haven't studied.

—Charlie Wadsworth, Orlando Sentinel

A Minneapolis second grader has a hero in the assistant postmaster who, the boy insists, "looks just like Abraham Lincoln."

His teacher asked what the resemblance might be. "He is tall and has big feet," the child explained.

—Minneapolis Tribune

Educators like a story about two first graders standing outside school one morning. "Do you think," asked one, "that thermonuclear projectiles will pierce the heat barrier?"

"No" said the second. "Once a force enters the substratosphere . . "

Then the bell rang. Said the first: "There goes the bell. Darn it, now we gotta go in and string beads."

—Carl Bernstein, Parade

The teacher was organizing the first graders for their lunch period. "Will all the boys and girls who will have hot lunches in the cafeteria stand over here, please. And will all those who have brought their lunch buckets stand over there."

The two groups quickly separated except for one bewildered boy. "Teacher," he asked, "where do the bags go?"

—Wisconsin Journal of Education

Our six-year-old daughter, Dala Dee, was eager to enter first grade. On the day before the opening of school, she heard some older neighbor children singing "School Days." Evidently she misinterpreted one phrase, for after her first day at school she came home somewhat disconsolate. Upon being questioned, she revealed the reason. "Well," she explained, "I didn't get any licorice. I heard some of the other children singing, "School days, school days. good old golden rule days, reading and writing and 'rithmetic. taught to the tune of a licorice stick."

—M. Dale Baughman

On the first day of school in Frederick, Oklahoma, a first-grade teacher told her students her full name—first and last—and told them to call her by whatever name they chose.

One of the students, Barry Hardin, told his father about it.

"What did you call her, son?" asked the father, the Rev. Mart Hardin.

"Fatso," said Barry.

—George Dolan,
Ft. Worth Star-Telegram, Comedy and Comment

Miss Tweedle was quite shocked when she found a puddle on the floor of the first grade coat hall. She announced to the class her discovery but being a firm believer in progressive teaching methods, promised them that no one would be punished. "What we'll all do " she continued sweetly, "is bow our heads and close our eyes for ten minutes. At the end of that period, I'll go into the coat hall and the puddle will be mopped up."

So all the sweet little tykes, along with Miss Tweedle, closed their eyes and at the end of ten minutes, she arose and strode confidently into the coat hall. Sure enough, the little puddle was gone. But down at the far end of the coat hall was a new puddle, with a piece of paper stuck on the wall above it. On the paper was a scribbled note. It said:

"The phantom strikes again!"

—Unknown

The first grader was describing her recent appendectomy to her classmates: 'They told me it wouldn't hurt, and then they stuck a needle in my arm and I disappeared."

—*The Education Digest*

Teacher Jan McKeithen was discussing etiquette with her first graders. "And do you know why we must cover our mouths when we yawn?" sh asked. "Yes," replied one bright lad, "to keep our bubble gum from falling out."

—Red O'Donnell, *Nashville Banner*

The first grader asked his mother why his father brought home a briefcase of material each night. When the mother replied, "Daddy has so much to do that he can't finish it all at the office so he has to work at night," the boy asked, "Well, why don't they just put him in a slower group?"

—Dr. Myron Wegman, *Education Digest, Quote*

The seven-year-old lad had a frown on his face as he started for school. His mother stopped him. "Son," she softly urged, "put a smile on your face and have a happy day."

After school, the lad returned home. His face was one big frown.

"What happened?" asked mom. "I thought you were going to smile and have a happy day."

The lad shook his head. "That don't work, mom. I tried to keep smiling, but the teacher thought I was up to something and was on my neck most of the day."

—*Council Bluffs Nonpareil, Comedy and Comment*

PTA

The heavy snowstorms had closed the schools for a week. One harried mother of seven school-age children said to a neighbor, "If they don't reopen school tomorrow, I'm going to burn my PTA card."

—Unknown

A Texas psychiatrist is lecturing to PTA groups in Dallas and Houston on the subject, "Alaska: How to explain it to your child."

—Frances Benson

REPORT CARDS

The question of cheating was being discussed in school just before an examination. "Miss Jones, what do you think of cheating?" one of the students asked. In a soft tone, the teacher replied, "If you can cheat and live with yourself, that's your business."

Next day the report cards were sent home. Upon returning his,

a gangling youth said, "Miss Jones, I find that I can cheat and live
with myself much better than I can fail and live with my mother."

—Laugh Book

Little boy (showing father his report card): "Remember how
proud you were when you got a golf score under 80? Well, look at
this spelling score."

—Current Science, Quote

A ten-year-old came home from school with a failing report
card, and painfully took it to his parents. Aghast, his father ranted
and raved, and ended up by saying that when he had been in
school he had never come close to failing a grade. "Well,"
philosophized the youngster, "let's not say I failed; let's just say
they failed to pick up my option for the fifth grade."

—Quote

A teacher had the son of the town's outstanding citizen and
banker in her class. The boy cheated constantly in his daily work
and on his examinations. Afraid to be blunt with his father, she
finally wrote this remark on his report card: "Forging his way
steadily ahead."

— Education Courier, Quote

A fifth-grade boy brought home a dreary report card for which
he felt neither apologetic nor chastened. However, he sought
vengeance on the teacher by listing some questions which he
would like to ask her. He added, "I'll bet she doesn't know the
answers to some of these." The list included:

—How can you tell a Ford Station Wagon from a Studebaker
  Station Wagon from the rear?
—What is the horsepower of a Caterpillar Bulldozer, Model D-8?
—How do you feed a pet snapping turtle?
—How long does it take to dismantle and reassemble an alarm
  clock?
—What is a Phillips screwdriver?
—What is the best way to start a car when the starter is stuck?
—When does the infield fly rule in baseball apply?

The youth added, "There are some questions that are easy for
me to answer."

—Unknown

Lady down the block is going around smiling and telling folks that the city is employing much better teachers. Junior came home with a good report card.

—Hugh Allen, *Knoxville News Sentinel*

Some people say the younger generation isn't considerate. This is an error, as a Memphis mother who suffers occasional migraine misery can testify. Only the other day her nine-year-old son came home from school as quiet and subdued and polite as all get out. He rummaged around in his books and brought out his report card. She held out her hand. He extended it to her, and then drew it back. "You know," he said with tender concern, "I kinda hate to show you this, because I know you're going to get one of those minor headaches."

—Lydel Sims, *Memphis Commercial Appeal*

A teen-ager complained to a friend: "My dad wants me to have all the things he never had when he was a boy—including five A's on my report card."

—*Today's Chuckle*

"Can I help you, son?" asked the proprietor of this small stationery store of a youngster who had been leafing through the establishment's entire stock of greeting cards for some time.

The kid nodded gravely.

"Just what are you looking for, Sonny?" asked the proprietor. "Birthday greetings? An anniversary card for your mother and father?"

The youngster shook his head and answered wistfully, "Do you have any blank report cards?"

—Gene Brown, *Danbury News-Times*

When the teacher asked my nephew where the Red Sea was, he replied, "It's on the second line of my report card."

—C. Ray Erler

A mother was studying her son's report card trying to figure out how he got a D in deportment at the same time he got an A in courtesy.

Finally, shaking her head, she said, "I guess it means that when he beats somebody up, he apologizes to him."

—*Sunshine Magazine*

A 15-year-old was discussing her report card. "No wonder Jean always gets an A in French," she observed. "Her father and mother speak French at the table."

"If that's the case," her boyfriend said, "I ought to get an A in geometry. My parents talk in circles!"

—Sunshine Magazine

Joe Crow Says: High grades don't really measure the student's intelligence, but low grades accurately test his parents' patience.

—Unknown

Quoth father to son, "I'll tell you why I signed your report with an X. With grades like yours, I don't want any teacher to think you've got a father who can read or write."

—Weldon Owens, *Dallas Times Herald*

Called upon to account for a bad report card, a fourth-grade boy explained to his father, "No wonder I seem stupid to the teacher—she's a college graduate!"

—Contemporary Education

The teachers' bulletin from a Toronto, Canada, high school offers definitions in plain English for tactful remarks that may be noted on a student's report cards. Such as:

"Shows difficulty in distinguishing between imaginary and factual material."*—He lies.*

"Needs ample supervision in order to work well."*—He's lazy.*

"Needs guidance in developing good habits of hygiene."*—He's dirty.*

"Has qualities of leadership but needs help in learning to use them democratically."*—He's a bully.*

—Capt. Tom L. Gibson, *Sunshine Magazine*

Man mentioned that his son's report card was terrible, "But at least it proved he wasn't taking any mind-expanding drugs."

—Herb Rau,
The Miami News, Comedy and Comment

The current system of school grading is designed not to discourage any parent or student. Even though Junior may be dumber than an ox, the idea is to hold out some encouragement.

Ultimate in strained encouragement came when one teacher

added this note to what was otherwise a very poor report: "He contributes nicely to the group singing by helpful listening."

—Unknown

The giant tackle was most dismayed by the results shown on his semester report card. Taking the card to his friend the coach, he said, "Gee, coach, what am I gonna do?"

"Now sit down, Moose," said the coach. "Let's look this thing over."

With furrowed brow the coach studied the card intently. "Well, it says you got a D and three F's—looks to me, Moose, like you been putting too much time on one subject."

—"Rotary Wheel," Refugio, Texas *Rotarian*

A lawyer's wife was telling Judge Tom Stovall of her folly in urging her son, who has just begun the first grade, to make all A's in school. Several times during the summer, she said, she told the boy that making A's was every pupil's goal.

The boy seemed a little put out when he came home from his second day at school. His mother asked what was wrong.

"I told my teacher you said to make nothing but A's," he said, "but she still wants me to learn to make B's and C's and all the rest, too."

—George Fuermann, *Houston Post*

Daddy was praising Janie for getting A in conduct on her first report card. Janie glowed with pride, then asked: "Would it be all right if I got B next time and had a little fun?"

—*Watchman-Examiner*

Parents, are you bewildered by those comments the teacher writes on your youngster's report card? With the help of college professors and the school janitor, I succeeded in translating them. Following are typical teacher comments and their translations:

Michael does not socialize well.
(This means Mike is always beating some other kid's brains out.)

John is progressing very well for him.
(Don't feel so happy, pappy—this means Johnny is a dope. He's 12 years old and has just learned 2 and 2 make 4, which, as teacher points out, is progress—for him.)

Frank's personality evidences a lack of social integration.
(This is a nice way of saying Frank is a stinker.)

Oscar shows a regrettable lack of self-control.
(This means Oscar doesn't do what teacher wants. Self-control means how much control the teacher has over Oscar.)

Henry seems emotionally immature for the first grade.
(Get out little Hank's birth certificate, mother—this means that teacher thinks you lied about his age to get him in school.)

Jerome participates very fully in class discussions.
(This may be good or bad. It means that Jerry never shuts his big yap. Perhaps he'll grow up to be a salesman.)

James is an individualist.
(Another nice way of saying James is a troublemaker.)

Richard's work indicates a lack of mastery over the upper ranges of the fundamental combinations necessary for arithmetical computation.
(Don't rush to a psychiatrist, just teach Dick his 7, 8 and 9 tables—he doesn't know them.)

David does not harmonize well with peer group.
(This has nothing to do with his voice. Teacher means that he can't get along with his classmates. Or, everybody in the class is out of step but Davey boy.)

Nathan's lack of muscular coordination prevents him from participating fully in body-building activities.
(Cut down on the calories, mom—Nate's too fat to play games.)

Robert is a well-adjusted, wholesomely integrated individual.
(Jackpot, brother, you're in. Bobby is teacher's Pet!)

—Al Barandon, *Philadelphia Inquirer*

"All that criticism of the American school system in the newspapers and magazines is completely justified!" exclaimed a teen-age girl just home from school.

"Do you really think so?" asked her mother.

"I certainly do! And if you want proof of how bad it is, just look at the terrible marks on this report card!"

—Comedy and Comment

Youngster to father examining his report card: "I am not an under-achiever. My teacher is an over-expecter."

—Bob Goddard,
St. Louis Globe Democrat, Comedy and Comment

Youngster, handing report card to his parents: "Look this over and see if I can sue for defamation of character."

—Philnews, quoted in *Omaha World-Herald*

Asked why she hadn't brought home a report card, a certain nine-year-old individual I know replied, "Maybe they haven't got enough on me yet."

—Ashley Cooper, *Charleston News and Courier*

The son had nothing but D's on his report card. "Time," his mother told his dad, "to tell him about the A's and B's."

—T.O. White, *Tow Lines*

---RESEARCH---

Only recently, foresters learned a substance they were using as an extinguisher was actually speeding up the rate of burning. This kind of experience has brought out the need for further research, they said.

—Unknown

A meeting was set for next week of the Technical Sub-Committee to evaluate plans for the initial study in what is anticipated will be a chain or sequence of pilot studies leading up to a major study in which several measurement methods will be compared simultaneously.

—Press release from the
Radio Advertising Bureau, New York

Much of what passes for research today is the alignment of data in orderly piles, hallowed by sacred hymns sung to the goddess Objectivity in the shrine of Statistics.

—William B. Bean

Some research has come in for criticism lately on the grounds that it doesn't produce anything new or important. Take the work of a Cornell University researcher, Prof. Harold Feldman, who studied 800 married couples. Married men, he finds, become constantly meeker, quieter, less demanding. Married women become more talkative and aggressive. So, professor, what's new?

—*Milwaukee Journal*

Government bureaus succeed in keeping more and more people "busy" these days in making available information. For example, a study just completed at a cost of $1,400 and 300 man hours gives us this stirring information: The average man's posterior covers 179.4 square inches, and exerts an average pressure of .92 pound per square inch.

We are confident this information will add measurably to the gross national economy, and raise our standard of living to an all-time high.

—Lennox (S.D.) *Independent*

Recent research from a prominent institute reports that parenthood is hereditary. If your parents didn't have children, the chances are you won't either.

—Today's Chuckle

Research shows that tall men are just as short at the end of the month as anybody else.

—Today's Chuckle

———————————— SCHOOL ACTIVITIES ————————————

As a young lad he had always been taught at home to say good things about people, never to make remarks if they were true which might embarrass people or make them feel inadequate. He learned his lessons well.

At his first school dance the turn of events found him dancing with a quite plump young lady. At first he was speechless, but his home training came to his rescue as he politely complimented his partner, "You sweat less than any fat girl I ever danced with."

—Unknown

During the school assembly, the Glee Club began to warble out, "When Irish eyes are smiling." In the middle of the song, a woman began to cry.

"I didn't know you were Irish," one of the teachers said, comforting her.

"I'm not," the teacher sobbed. "I'm the new music teacher."

—Sunshine Magazine

Quite a few of the boys were excused from school early on the day of the senior prom. They were having their hair done.

−Quote

The Old Paragrapher can remember away back when there were more members of any varsity athletic team, even the basketball team, than cheerleaders.

−Unknown

──────── SCHOOL ADMINISTRATORS–SCHOOL BOARDS ────────

Secretary to secretary: "We call him the office locomotive. All he does is run back and forth, smoke and whistle."

Quote

A generation ago I ran to be a board member in Arkansas at the request of the county superintendent. I was at the time a small-town superintendent. I ran against a one-armed man. And that is my first suggestion to you board members. Don't run against a one-armed man. I just barely won.

I knew the late Senator Barkley, and he had some very good stories. One of his best was about politics down in Hickman County, Kentucky. The candidates were going around over the country to appear together on the platform for a few minutes and say why they should be elected. In this particular race there were three. The first was a one-armed man, and he explained why he, a one-armed man, ought to have the job.

The second man was one-legged. He made a big to-do about that. The third and final candidate, the one who had two arms and two legs as everybody could see, broke out in a cold sweat. Finally, in desperation, he got up and said, "Ladies and gentlemen, I didn't know it was going to be settled on the grounds of physical disability, but if it is, I just want you to know I am the damn worst ruptured man in all Hickman County."

−Henry H. Hill, President Emeritus,
George Peabody College for Teachers

What they write:	*What they mean:*
"Our citizenship-in-action program is now in full bloom. . . "	"Once a year pupils are asked to pick up paper and trash from the school grounds."
"We have re-oriented our curriculum to the hard realities of the space age."	"A memorandum from the central office suggested that science teachers try to develop a new unit on 'The New Age of Space' if they can squeeze it into the recommended course of study."
"Our school construction program has been adjusted to the needs of our school population and the wishes of the community."	"All multi-purpose rooms have been eliminated from the building plans because a local pressure group raised a ruckus about these fancy facilities which don't look like old fashioned classrooms."

—Unknown

Chairman of the board to other members: "Of course, it's only a suggestion, gentlemen, but let's not forget who's making it."

—*The RoTooTor,* Daytona Beach, Florida

See the man!
He superintends the whole school system.
He is called a superintendent.
See his bulging eyes. Funny.
See his red face. Funny.
Hear his funny stomach churn
Churn, churn, churn.
The super has a funny ulcer.
Many supers have funny ulcers
But some supers do not have funny ulcers.
They have funny high blood pressure.

—Unknown

See the bright and shiny school buildings!
Many nice teachers and superintendents work here.

Let us count the superintendents.
Count, count, count! Hmmm! Several supts are missing.
Some more referenda must have failed.
Dear, dear, dear, where are the nice superintendents now?
At the nice Educational Placement Office.
Sign, sign, sign.
Isn't job security nice in schoolville?

                                                    —Unknown

School administration is easier than you think. It requires nothing more than to undertake the impossible, forego the indispensable and bear the intolerable.

                                                    —Unknown

Sir,

In these times of salary negotiations perhaps a note of humor would be appreciated by some of our committees and by school board committees.

Last fall while we were in the midst of our negotiations here, the local board, as has been its custom for some years, kindly invited all administrators and teachers new to our area to a very pleasant social function.

I had been detailed to organize some entertainment in which I included some community singing. During this activity I offered various "dignitaries," including principals and board members, a chance to name a tune for us to sing together. Mr. Hugh Anderson, who was, and still is, chairman of the board came up with song number 72, "Side by Side." You can imagine the reaction this brought when we looked at the first line in the song, which reads: "We Ain't Got a Barrel of Money."

                            —Alfred B. Price, *The B C Teacher*

Every school administrator, according to some jokesters, now needs three assistants: one to write proposals and explain to state and federal bureaucrats what changes are about to be made; another to tell the board of education, the community, and the teachers that the changes won't make any difference; and a third to attend meetings called by the first two.

                       —H. Thomas James, *Education Digest, Quote*

I heard about a new way of classifying administrators the other day. According to this source there are just four types of executives:

The ULCEROIDAL type goes around worrying all the time. Whereas the ADENOIDAL one yells constantly, the THYROIDAL rushes here and there loaded with purposeless pep, and the HEMORRHOIDAL one just sits and sits on the situation and waits for it to clear up.

—Unknown

School boards have a tough job these days—monitoring the length of girls' dresses and the boys' hair, and guarding them against catching religion.

Undertaker Tells Truth in Grave Story:

Pittsburg, Kansas, Sept. 28 (AP)—Tom Bath, president of the Pittsburg school board, in the first faculty meeting of the school year here, was assuring the pedagogues of the loyalty of the school board members. He said in closing:

"You can be sure about at least two board members. They will be the last to let you down."

Bath and another board member, Chester Ward, are undertakers.

—Unknown

From the Dayton, Ohio, *Journal Herald:* "The Kettering school board, meeting for the first time since the defeat of the $4,950,000 school bond issue, agreed to defer for several months a decision on what to do now."

> See the kindly old man.
> He is president of the school board.
> He has fired nine superintendents,
> Fire, fire, fire.
> See the fine young man with him.
> He will not be fired.
> He's a fine school man.
> He is the fine assistant superintendent.
> He is a fine nephew of the president of the board.

—Mad Magazine

"John," implored a harried homemaker, "get up and get ready for school or you'll be late."

John: "No, I don't want to go today. The bus driver hates me. He talks about me all the time."

She called again two minutes later. "John, get up, you'll be late for school."

John: "No, I'm not ready yet. I don't want to go to school. The kids talk about me behind my back and the bus driver dislikes me."

A third time she cried out for John to get out of bed and prepare for school.

"No," he objected, "the teachers don't accept me, the kids talk about me and the bus driver doesn't like me. Nobody likes me."

"John," she begged, "get up; you're 45 and the principal of that school. Get up and go."

—Unknown

The principal is hoping something is done about all this highjacking before the idea catches on with the kids riding the school bus.

—Tom Eilerts, *Kansas City* (Mo.) *Times*

Some parents are still wondering if the principal was speaking from experience or merely had a slip of the tongue. At the first PTA meeting he introduced the faculty to them, saying, "These are the teachers your children will educate this year."

—*Mississippi Educational Advance*

Mickey Porter says, "In the old days if a kid was in the principal's office it meant the kid was in trouble. Now it means the principal's in trouble."

—Leo Aikman, *Atlanta Constitution*

The principal of an Iowa junior high school penned a note to his teachers which read in part: "It's the same old story. Some students are still doing poor work because of failure to get needed hell after 3:30 p.m." However, alongside the statement, he wrote in appropriate red ink: "My stenographer hit the wrong key. The word should be help."

—Unknown

A school principal had finally retired after some 40 years of catching the 7:30 a.m. train. The first morning at breakfast, when his wife placed his plate in front of him, he said he wished she would not turn his fried eggs over as he didn't like them that way.

"My dear," she exclaimed, "why didn't you ever tell me?"

"I never had time before," he replied.

—*Quote*

I suppose one principal, who's retiring, won't be missed much. "They gave him the farewell party during a coffee break."

—"Today's Best Laugh," *Indianapolis News*

Some time ago, the president of a school board asked me to write the specifications for a high school principalship, there being one coming into vacancy in that community. The longer I thought of it, the clearer it became to me that I could sum up the whole requirement by writing that it would be useful in the candidate's past if he had been a kamikaze pilot.

Harold Gores, *NASSP Bulletin, Quote*

There was a motion to fire the principal when it came out that half the kids in school had test scores below the school average.

—Unknown

From the endorsement of a Korean boy by his principal: ". . . he has an extinguished ability in math and science."

—Unknown

The principal of a military academy, recommending an applicant: "His interests are scholastic, which has a tendency to set him apart."

Unknown

A principal while at a convention met some other principals from apparently more affluent school districts. Discovering that his annual salary was considerably less than theirs, he immediately wired the school board president. "Must have raise at once or count me out."

Back came a simple telegram in reply: "One, two, three, four, five, six, seven, eight, nine, and ten."

—Unknown

A good supervisor is one who knows how to step on your toes and not mess up your shine.

Sunshine Magazine

Supervision: "How to be Successful" (Without Really Trying)

Welcome to the club: You are about to become initiated into the cult of negativism. You cannot assume the role of a charter member as the club is already well established. The rules are simple. If you are intrigued with the idea of becoming a member, simply adhere to the eight steps listed below for your convenience:

Always frown when asked for help. This will assure your colleagues that you are too busy to assist them with their problems. They must be made to realize that your job involves budget preparation, evaluation of teachers, classroom visitations, mountains of papers to be processed, and a myriad of other details which are keeping you so busy that your coffee breaks are beginning to suffer.

Assure people that you have all the answers. Never hesitate to propose a better answer to the problem which is causing a teacher much worry and distress. It is obvious that someone so intimately involved cannot look at the problem as objectively as one who is on the scene for the first time and clearly sees all the various facets involved in the dilemma. The old adage, "Always criticize, it makes you look like an expert," cannot be overlooked. If staff members are doing a good job, find something to criticize and quickly provide a ready-made answer to the problem. Be sure to emphasize the fact that you followed this procedure when you were teaching and it always worked for you. This will build self-confidence on the part of the staff members and they will look to you as a vital source of information.

Never ask others for suggestions. You were placed in a position of responsibility and authority based on your successful teaching experience, qualities of leadership, organizational ability, and knowledge of the subject. Qualifications such as these leave little room for improvement. It is generally advisable to remain aloof from staff members and colleagues, for "familiarity breeds contempt." You are constantly beset with problems only you can solve, and working too closely with colleagues may encourage them to discuss their problems with you. They may also feel compelled to offer ideas regarding procedures, curriculum changes, or items to be placed on the agenda at department meetings. They may not realize that your agenda always includes items of major importance.

Shrug off, as unimportant, requests from subordinates. Your philosophy must be one of putting first things first. There are teachers who will insist on asking for additional equipment, more money in the budget, emergency supplies, or clarification regarding transportation arrangements for an appearance away from school. These must be viewed in the proper perspective. Teachers tend to panic over relatively unimportant details. You must keep in mind that what you are doing in the office is of prime importance. The success or failure of the instructional program is not dependent on the contributions of staff members. Your work is more important. Remember, first things first.

Refrain from specifics in conversations with colleagues. Cultivate the ability to talk in generalities and to avoid giving direct answers to questions posed by staff members. You should be prepared to steer the conversation away from the problem by shifting the discussion to a recent article or book you have read which is not necessarily related to the subject at hand. Discussions which are centered around specifics tend to force you into a position of making decisions when needed. You should have ample time to gather pertinent facts and give sufficient thought to the problem. Vague answers tend to perpetuate problems, thus assuring you of a busy schedule in the future.

Carry your feelings "on your sleeve." Don't be guilty of sparing the feelings of staff members if you feel they are not "getting the job done." This will avoid creating a false sense of security on the part of colleagues who are experiencing difficulties. A good teacher can solve any problem regardless of experience or conditions. If you have had a bad morning at the office, don't appear too relaxed or pleasant later in the day. You have a tough job. Your staff should be aware of this fact. Your conduct will help them appreciate the problems you face daily at the office.

Always keep those with appointments waiting and periodically have them postponed. This will keep staff members conscious of your busy schedule and of the many details you must conquer each day. Avoiding specifics will enhance the possibility of using more than the allotted time for appointments. Postponements always leave people convinced that you are both overworked and underpaid for what you are doing.

Cultivate the habit of procrastinating. This will enable you to avoid meeting deadlines, making unpleasant decisions, or keeping appointments. By so doing, you will always appear to be so busy that you don't have time to talk with colleagues about concerns of vital interest to them.

These rules should cover most situations. If they seem too detailed or cumbersome, the following general principles may suffice: Keep standards low, be more impressed with quantity than quality, avoid aggressive leadership, and promote the status quo.

Take a close look at what you are doing. Are you following the rules stated in the preceding paragraphs? If your work is reflected by the criteria described above, you are serving as a supervisor—without really trying! Consider yourself duly initiated. Welcome to the club!

> —Wilburn Elrod, *Contemporary Education*. Used with permission.

Students who refuse to act their age may find themselves confronted with school authorities who have finally decided to act theirs.

> Frank Reynolds, *TV Newsman*

After the Supreme Court ruling the principal of one elementary school had the praying mantis removed from the sixth-grade insect display.

> Unknown

---------------------------------- SCHOOL ----------------------------------

Eric, a first grader, commented at dinner one night that a certain boy in his class was not progressing to the teacher's satisfaction in his Think and Do book. When asked what the boy was doing wrong, Eric said, "Well, he do's and then thinks."

> *The Christian Science Monitor, Education Digest*

Some kids today are over-privileged. One in the cafeteria line the other day wanted to see the wine list.

> —Unknown

A parable for counselors: In one of Israel's Kibbutzim there was a donkey. It was a special donkey indeed, with long silky ears and large shiny eyes, and all the children loved him dearly.

And so when the donkey, whose name was Shlomo, disappeared one day, all the children were very upset. Their sadness was contagious, and before the day was out all the Kibbutz had assembled in the dining hall, trying to decide what to do next.

As they were bemoaning their loss, in walked an old man, somewhat senile and the object of ridicule in the Kibbutz, dragging Shlomo, the donkey, behind him. The jubilation was great, the astonishment even greater. While the children surrounded the donkey, the adults gathered around the old man. "How is it," they asked him "that you of all people have found the donkey? What did you do?"

The old man scratched his bald pate, looked at the ceiling and then at the floor, smiled, and said, "It was simple. I just asked myself, 'Shlomo [for that was the old man's name as well], if you were Shlomo, the donkey, where would you go off to?' So I went there and found him and brought him back."

—Houghton Mifflin *Sampler*

It is thoughtless of the commencement speaker to tell the graduates that the world outside now belongs to them and then keep them sitting there 45 minutes before they get a chance at it.

—Unknown

This is an excerpt from a letter written by a freshman girl up at the boarding school:

" . . . and I am gaining on this awful food they serve me at the dorm, too. I weigh 120 stripped, but I don't know whether those scales down in front of the drug store are right or not."

Laugh Book

The dean of a girls' school was troubled because the girls insisted on crossing the street in front of the school without going to the corner. Warnings, penalties, and lectures did no good. Finally, the dean had a sign painted and set it up in the middle of the block. From that time on, the girls always walked to the corner before crossing the street. What did the sign read? "Cattle Crossing."

The day after the circus came to town, a teacher of the first grade received the following excuse for the absence of one of her pupils:

"Dear teacher: Education, you know, is a lot of things. It is reading and writing and ciphering. It is 'Yes, please' and 'Yes, thanks,' and 'No, thank you.' It is the washing of our hands and the use of forks. It is pencils and scissors and paste and erasers and chalk dust. It is the smell of a school room early Monday morning.

It is the excitement of vacations. It is autumn bonfires and sleds and puddle-wading.

"Yes, education is a lot of things. It is a brass band blaring and a calliope tootling. Education is a woman shot from a cannon, a man on a tight rope, a seal playing a tune with his nose. It is sideshow barkers, clowns, lions, cotton candy, cowboys and spangles. Education is the wonderment of new things and new sensations. It is, in short, a circus.

"That's why Ginger wasn't in your classroom yesterday. Excuse it, please."

—Unknown

One dad told his son he walked five miles to school as a youngster, all uphill, both ways.

Comedy and Comment

News item in school paper: "Mr. Brown visited the school yesterday and lectured on destructive pests. A large number were present."

Elizabeth Meyer, Herndon, Virginia

We are more careful about transporting our china tea cups than we are about how we bus our children.

Ralph Nader, *Quote*

A fourth grader read in a newspaper that a Greyhound driver was going to retire after two million miles on a bus. "What's so great about that?" he asked his father. "Shucks, the way things are going, I'll have that many in by the time I get to junior high."

Comedy and Comment

Kids have it tough. Where they used to walk to school and keep warm by running part of the way, now they stand and shiver waiting for the bus.

—Claude Eames, *Elkhorn* (Wis.) *Independent*

One small schoolboy to another: "It might be unconstitutional, but I always pray before a test."

Reamer Keller, *McCall's*

Mary had a little prayer,
She said it every day,
But when she has her lunch at school,
Her prayer she must not say.

It makes some grown-ups much disturbed
When children pray at school,
The highest court in all the land
Was asked to make a rule.
And so in Mary's fine, new school
No prayers shall be said;
Why, there are some who boldly say
That Mary's God is dead!
But Mary, wiser than them all,
Believes God knows and cares,
She bows her head and silently
Still offers him her prayers.

Irma Harem, *Quote*

An article by Karen Scheidies in the Hastings, Nebraska, High School "Tiger Cub" began thus:

"Let's elope during the lunch hour."

"What?" Agnes was stunned. She hadn't realized that things had gotten that serious. "But I couldn't possibly. I might get a detention slip."

"Then how about after school?" Alfred asked.

"We have a pep club meeting," Agnes countered.

Alfred was crushed, "You don't really want to marry me, do you?"

"No, quite frankly, I don't."

Desperation overcame him. "I'll commit suicide. I'll eat in the cafeteria."

Comedy and Comment

Hear about the kid who dropped out of school because they didn't have a place he could plug in his electric eraser.

Comedy and Comment

What is a School Lunch?
—In the primary grades it is a threat: "You can't go out to play until you eat."
—In the elementary grades it's a contest: "My plate's clean first; can I have my seconds now?"
—In the high school it's a tool for asserting new-found sophistication: "I can't eat this slop."
—In the faculty room it's a wail: "If I eat it I'll get fat."

—In the kitchen it's a worry: "Will they like it today?"

—To the manager it's a challenge: "How can I make it on this budget?"

To the federal government it's a type A meal: One glass of milk, two ounces of a protein, 3/4 cup of fruit or vegetable, bread and butter.

—To a busy mother, it's a blessing.

The Westcovinian

Inky Stebbens reports he overheard a couple of ladies bragging about their progeny recently and one of then sniffed at the other: "My son dropped out of a better school than your son."

Unknown

A sign on a New York subway read: "Don't be like me. I were a school drop-out."

Some wag had scribbled underneath, "Not me. I goed on to college."

Unknown

Ever since the first sputnik was sent up we have put pressure on our students, made longer assignments, required more homework, lengthened the school term and the school day and discussed a six-day school week. Meanwhile adults clamor for the 35-hour week, more vacations, coffee breaks and fringe benefits.

Small wonder that we have high school dropouts. The adult world appears so much easier.

—Unknown

I was seated next to the superintendent on the stage at commencement exercises one spring night in a central Illinois farming community, the hub of which was a small town of 700 people. I was waiting to give the main address. Exactly at 9:00 p.m. a siren sounded loud and clear. I turned to the superintendent on my left and asked, "Do you suppose there's a fire?" "No," he explained, "Once there was a 9:00 p.m. curfew here and they have never stopped sounding the siren at that hour."

—M. Dale Baughman

Dr. Ralph Peterson reminds us that school is the mouse race that equips you for the rat race.

—Will Jones, *Minneapolis Tribune*

Schools are built on pillars of contrast. They are homes, playgrounds, and jails for men, women and children, young and old. They are institutions supported by parents and condemned by taxpayers.

They are full of laughter, corny jokes, guilty consciences, books, rulers, kids, bells, janitors, uncomfortable furniture, test tubes, excuses, regulations, and a little learning.

They smell of paste, oiled floors, gym suits, hydrogen sulphide, lunches, radiators and children.

They shelter people who wear snow-suits, shoulder pads, sneakers, evening gowns, worn-out saddle shoes, dungarees, loose shirts, lipstick and gold footballs.

School is a place that kids live to get into; then die to get out of. It starts too early in September and ends too late in June.

It abounds with kids with runny noses, boys without homework and girls who like to hold hands. It is the only place where students can be heard and not seen, and where kids get sick on the first day of fishing season.

It is the building where students forget to put their names on paper but remember to put them on everything else.

Yet it vibrates with warmth and understanding, love and devotion, and grandstands of cheers. It is the place that folks think back upon with a flush of pride when they say, "I went to school in Toms River."

—Louis Albini, *Bulletin,*
Wisconsin Association of Sec. School Principals

Mil: "You say your great-grandfather always got out of school early. How come?"

Phil: "He put quicksand in the hour glass."

—Unknown

A 12-year-old boy defines the phrase "mixed emotions": "It's like hearing the morning siren telling you that school is closed because of a blizzard—and you are in bed with the flu."

—*Fraternal Monitor, Quote*

Progressive schools are where they never do anything to bruise a child's ego. One kid played hookey for three months but they never called it that. They just said he flunked roll call!

—Unknown

Suburban friends were startled the other day when their youngster brought a note home from school. Both his teacher and his principal wanted a written excuse for his presence!

Teachers College Record

Prayer should never be taken out of the public schools. That's the only way a lot of us got through.

Grit

Then there's the story about the kid who was kept in after school. He was caught praying.

Quote

Educators are only beginning to appreciate students like the 15-year-old boy who wrote his counselor, "I'm awfully sorry I still have only B grades. But this year I read all of Shakespeare, and I was so busy learning that I just didn't have time to do all my school work."

T.F. James, "What Makes a Creative Child?"
This Week Magazine

Another definition of classroom restlessness is "squirm warfare."

The Education Digest

On a school bulletin board—"Free. Wisdom on Mondays through Fridays. Bring your own container."

Quote

No wonder teachers don't keep pupils after school any more. If the kid misses his school bus, you have to buy him a return ticket on the Greyhound line.

—Bill Gold, *Washington Post*

Personal history from the pupils' own reports: "My IQ is 20/20." "Blood type: Irish." "I had to go to the dentist as I had loose morals."

The Education Digest

Doug Haney says you may as well let most drivers pass you on the freeway. "They'll pass you in the next school zone anyway," he adds.

—Paul Crum, *Dallas Morning News*

One of the biggest jobs that schools face is getting money from the taxpayers without disturbing the voters.

Quote

The Dawson County (Ga.) Board of Education has adopted a dress code which demands among other things:

"All students, regardless of sex, shall wear the hair in such a manner that will make the eyes fully visible at all times. . ."

Well, that seems reasonable enough.

After all, how can you teach if you can't see the pupils!

—Leo Aikman, *Atlanta Constitution*

──────────────────── SPORTS ────────────────────

Coach Pepper Roney says the old school football team won't be up to snuff this season, since his recruiting budget was caught in the wage-price freeze.

Comedy and Comment

Did you hear about that one football player SIU had? He's been in college nine years. It's a sad, sad, story. He can run and he can kick but he can't pass.

—Unknown

A young man hoping to enter a California University on a football scholarship was discussing his prospects with an acquaintance. Asked if he had submitted his high school transcript, he said, "Oh, yes. The college authorities are overlooking my marks right now."

—Bill Hall, *San Francisco Examiner*

They tell me a story about a young man who applied for work at the first store of Sebastian S. Kresge, of five-and-dime fame. Mr. Kresge said, "All right, son. Start by sweeping the store." The young man protested. "But I'm a college graduate!" Mr Kresge replied: "Then watch me and I'll show you how."

—*Quote*

Sul Ross College's basketball team had lost 17 games in a row. Then Sul Ross beat Texas A & I by 9 points.

And, two nights later, Sul Ross beat Southwest Texas State by 2 points, in a thriller.

At game's end, a happy fan raced over to Sul Ross coach Gerald Stockton and exclaimed: "Boy, I bet you were nervous, weren't you?"

"Of course not," Stockton replied. "I'm used to winning."

—George Dolan, *Ft. Worth Star Telegram*

Oklahoma City University basketball players are wearing a red shoe on one foot and a blue shoe on the other. Explains coach Abe Lemons: "We wanted to be first in something."
—Fred Russel, Nashville Banner, Comedy and Comment

"At the basketball games, I always pretend the referee is my wife and call him the things I'd like to call her, but don't have the nerve."
—Weldon Owens,
Dallas Times-Herald, Comedy and Comment

Abe Lemons, Oklahoma City University basketball coach, said one of his players was averaging 32 "half rebounds."

"That means he gets it off the board and somebody takes it away from him."
–Comedy and Comment

Jim Whatley, University of Georgia baseball mentor, went to school (Alabama) with Mel Allen, the famous announcer.

"As a freshman outfielder," vouchsafes Jim, "Mel would run in on a fly ball shouting, 'I've got it!' and then drop the ball. But Mel majored in English. When he was a senior, and better educated, he'd run in on a fly shouting, 'I have it!' then drop it."
Scholastic Coach

Lexington, Kentucky—"That was no zone . . . that was a stratified transitional hyperbolic paraboloid defense."

That is what Kentucky basketball Coach Adolph Rupp calls the formation used by his team to defeat Tennessee. Almost everybody else thought it was a zone.

But Rupp has despised the zone for years and has sworn his team would never use it.
Unknown

Joe Augustine wonders if you heard about the basketball team that lost so many games that the players gave the coaches a pep talk at half time. Attendance was so poor that the team hung the student body in effigy!
Buck Herzog, Milwaukee Sentinel

Gene Shields of Dallas was reminiscing to Jack Stroube about playing country basketball in West Texas when he was a kid.

The gym in his home town was made of green lumber, Shields said. It had cracks in the walls you could throw a cat through.

Shields said the only advice the coach ever gave was this: "When you line up for the center jump, take the wind."

George Dolan, Ft. Worth Star Telegram

A basketball coach (says Sam Pascal) had a wonderful dream: that a beautiful, rich girl lured him to her apartment—where he met her brother, who was seven feet tall.

Laugh Book

When Lawrence Central High School of Indiana lost its 36th straight game an exasperated fan wrote to the *Lawrence Journal* complaining that as a taxpayer who was helping to pay Coach Woodrow Crum's salary he didn't think he was getting his money's worth. Crum, who coached high school teams to the state finals three times before moving to Lawrence Central a few years ago, responded by dividing the number of taxpayers in Lawrence into his salary and then refunding the angry taxpayer his share: 6 cents. "It was just something I had to do," said Crum, whose team reacted by breaking the losing streak next time out.

Sports Illustrated, Quote

Distraught new father on phone: "But dear, what do I do now?"

Wife: "Just don't get excited. Got the diaper in front of you? All right. Now, that's a baseball diamond. Bring second base to home plate, lay the baby between first and third. Now bring first base, third base, and home plate together, and pin. Be sure to dust home plate with a little talcum. Simple, isn't it?"

The Lookout

You can tell the difference between football and baseball players, even in the locker room. The football players comb their hair, the baseball players shave.

—T.O. White, Tow Lines

She: "Why does the man behind the hitter wear such a big bib, honey? He looks silly."

He: "That, my dear, is to keep the catcher's shirt from getting all mussed up in case a ball happens to knock his teeth out."

Sunshine Magazine

Sandy Koufax told Sam Snead that baseball is a tougher game than golf. "A round bat and a fast-moving target calls for more skill than hitting a still ball with a square clubhead."

"Yep," replied Snead, "but when a golfer hits a foul ball, he has to get out there and play it."

Quote

Then there was the football coach who noted in his application for a new job: "We had a great season physically, spiritually, and mentally. Morale was high. We just didn't win any games."

Don Fraser, *Comedy and Comment*

The football player was none too bright, but he was very eager. He kept running up to the coach and pleading, "Aw, come on, coach, send me in. Please! C'mon, lemme go in. Just lemme get in there and show those guys how to win!"

The coach finally became tired of the boy's pleadings, so he said, "Stop bothering me! If you want to play so bad, go on across the field to your side and ask your coach to put you in the game."

Quote

Confused child after being fitted for a new white practice uniform for Y.M.C.A. little peewee football:

Mother's comment: "Now don't come home from practice with dirt all over that new uniform."

Father's comment: "That white uniform had better be dirty after practice or no more football for you, son."

–Unknown

Locker-room conversation: "The coach's wife says he was deeply insulted by a mindreader; he was only charged half price!"

–Unknown

Dr. James B. Conant and Admiral Hyman G. Rickover may have doubts about sport's role in the American educational system, but Texas does not. Next September there will be a new high school in Garland, Texas. It is now being built. It has no student body. It has no principal. It has no teachers. What it has is a football coach.

–Unknown

I shot a pass into the air;
It fell to earth I know not where.
And that is why I sit and dream
On the bench with the second team.

–*The Lookout*

The story possibly is apocryphal, but it reaches our trust-every-one ear from a fellow who knows his football backwards, forwards and sideways. And he swears it happened in the Wichita dressing room at half-time during the school's tussle with the Tulsa University Golden Hurricane.

One of Wichita's assistant coaches was belaboring a giant tackle about his lackadaisical play. "I want you to get back in there and fight!" the coach roared. "I want you to get rambunctious."

"Get who?" the tackle puzzled.

"Get rambunctious!" the coach repeated.

"Okay," the big boy said. "What's his number?"

—Roger Devlin, Tulsa Tribune

Good old Leon Cox, the football coach at Mclain High School, sent along one of those classics which kick around:

Dear Coach Musselman:

Remembering our discussions of your football men who were having troubles in English, I have decided to ask you, in turn, for help.

We feel that Paul Spingles, one of our most promising scholars, has a chance for a Rhodes scholarship, which would be a great thing for him and for our college.

Paul has the academic record for this award, but we find that the aspirant is required to have other excellences, and ideally should have a good record in athletics. Paul is weak. He tried hard, but he has troubles in athletics.

We propose that you give special consideration to Paul as a varsity player, putting him in the backfield if possible. In this way we can show a better college record to the Rhodes committee.

We realize Paul will be a problem, but as you have often said, cooperation between our departments is highly desirable.

His work in the English club and on the debate team will force him to miss many practices, but we will see that he carries an old football around to bounce (or whatever one does with a football) during intervals in his work.

We expect Paul to show entire good will in his work for you, and though he will not be able to begin football practice till late in the season, he will finish the season with good attendance.

Sincerely yours,
Ben Plotinss, Chairman,
English Department

—Comedy and Comment

Proud Mother: "Now, then, son, tell me—did you make the football team?"

Son: "No, mom. They already had one."

Quote

Then there was the golfer who was so used to cheating that when he made a hole-in-one he wrote down a zero.

Quote

There's a limit to almost anything except the number of wrong ways a golf ball can be hit.

Woodstock Sentinel-Review

"I play golf like James Bond. After every hole I yell, 'Oh, Oh, seven.' "

—Forrest Duke, *Las Vegas Review Journal*

Golf is a sport in which the ball usually lies poorly, but the player well.

The Rotonu, North Dekalb, Georgia

Golf pro: "Just go through the motions but don't hit the ball."
Beginner: "But that's the trouble I'm trying to cure!"

Quote

Near the end of a tense golf match, one contestant, very temperamental, was thrown off his game when his caddie developed a severe attack of hiccoughs. On the seventeenth hole he sliced his drive clean out of bounds and growled fiercely at the caddie, "That was on account of you and your blankety-blank hiccoughs."

"But I didn't hiccough then, sir," protested the caddie.

"That's just the point," screamed the player, "I had allowed for it!"

Quote

In a local high school locker, the coach taped this slogan to the wall: "Teamwork Is the Answer." Underneath, someone has Magic-Marked: "What Was the Question?"

—Bob Talbert, *Columbia State*

Bob Conibear, first-year basketball coach at Bowling Green, who disliked the officiating in his team's 90-88 double-overtime loss to St. Joseph's, described his sleep that night: "I dreamed I was on a safari in Africa and killed every zebra I saw."

—*Sports Illustrated, Quote*

Golf is flog spelled backwards.

—Troy Gordon, *Tulsa World*

Tiger Lyons is taking no chances with all that Thanksgiving football. "I invited the TV repairman to dinner."

—Robert J. Herguth,
Chicago Daily News, Comedy and Comment

From a Grenada, Mississippi, newspaper report on the festivities honoring Jake Gibbs at the time he signed a contract with the New York Yankees: "A parade of several bands preceded Jake to the football field, where he was presented a new car and many other lavish gifts to go with his $100,000 bonus. William S. Winters, state tax collector, served as master of ceremonies."

—Unknown

A famous basketball coach (and it is kinder not to mention him here) once bawled his team out at the half because they kept calling and shouting for passes from their teammates. "Be silent out there and work smoothly," he cautioned them. "Be mute—mutiny, that's what wins basketball games!"

—Unknown

Laconic report of a junior-high-school basketball game from the La Harpe, Illinois, *Quill:*

"The Terre Haute Flea-Weights defeated Colusa 13 to 2. Ted Kern was high score man for both teams, scoring 12 points for Terre Haute and two points at the wrong basket for Colusa."

—*Sports Illustrated*

As football season approaches, we are reminded of a high school football coach who explained his lack of success to a reporter.

"My real trouble with this year's squad," he said, "was the fact that most of my boys were too young and uncoordinated.

"As a matter of fact, I had one boy on the first string who was so uncoordinated that he couldn't walk and chew gum at the same time."

—Unknown

And now, with only two minutes left of this football game, I want to thank the fine spotters here in the booth with me, the fine engineers and producers, the fine coaches of both the fine teams of these two fine schools, the fine stadium custodians, and fine peanut vendors and the fine, fine, fine, fine. . .

—Unknown

Life will be lovely
This season, I guess
Provided the team
Has sufficient success.

Coaches work six days a week
Striving for precision,
Official quickly gums things
Up with single bum decision.

Halfbacks are agile and fragile
Fullbacks are brawny and stout,
Linemen galore are wide as a door
With holes where their teeth were knocked out.

—Bert McCrane, *The Coach*

If your golf score is higher than your IQ you are either a mighty poor golfer or extremely stupid.

—T.O. White, *Tow Lines*

Father: "How was your golf game today?"
Son: "Well, I am a little put out with my output of in-putts. It was not up to par."

—Harold D. Wiese

The pro football player complained to his coach, "I know you don't care much for the way I play but I don't think you should make me sit there on the bench during every game with that 'For Sale' sign hanging on my back."

Sunshine Magazine

Nebraska University's football coach, Bob Devaney, is known as the winningest coach in college football. But it wasn't always that way. He spent the first 13 years of his coaching career bouncing around four different Michigan high schools.

"My first coaching job was at Big Beaver High," he said. "The previous coach had a 0-40 record. They let him go because he overemphasized history. I was there two years and I kept his record intact."

—Fred Russel, *Nashville Banner*

"Whom are you happiest to see returning this year?" asked a writer at the start of a season. "Me," said former Coach Duffy

Daugherty of Michigan State. On another occasion, Duffy said, "We run the quadruple option play here. We hand the ball off, pitch it out, pass it or just let it lie there where we fumbled it."

—Furman Bisher,
Atlanta Journal, Comedy and Comment

A football coach, not particularly noted for coddling his players, was asked by a member of the faculty: "Why is it the boys don't love you the way they do other coaches?"

The rough and ready grid coach eyed the professor speculatively and replied: "Well, I guess I've been too busy coaching to do much courting."

Modern Maturity

A well-adjusted athlete is one who can play golf as if it were a game.

—Unknown

Tell the truth now. Did you ever figure to see the day when you tuned in a football game—and the cheerleaders looked over-dressed?

Current Comedy

—————————————— STUDENT MASTERPIECES ——————————————

A small boy approached the librarian and asked, "Do you have anything on the parent from 30 to 35?" He found something and, being a precocious youngster, wrote, "It is useless to try to change most parents. Studies of many cases show that this can rarely be done, even by other parents. However, life can be made much happier for everybody if we understand that most adults' behavior, however odd it may seem, is normal for that age and that they are going to behave that way anyway."

—Unknown

A small girl wrote the following composition on men: "Men are what women marry. They drink and smoke and swear, but don't go to church. They are more logical than women and also more zoological. Both men and women sprung from monkeys, but women sprung further than the men."

World Digest, Quote

Teachers come in many sizes and shapes—large, small, young, old, tired, fresh, black, white, rich, poor.

Some are kind, and some are not. Those who are mean are stinky. Some teachers know how to make you feel good; others make you feel bad all over, deep down. Some help you not to be afraid; others keep you scared all the time. Some show you what you might try; others tell you that you can't do it. They are no-no teachers. They're stinky. Lots of teachers go to college after they finish teaching you to see if they can learn some more. Some learn; some don't. Some it helps; some it don't. Those who don't try to learn and understand are stinky. Some teachers make you want to come to school every day; some teachers make you want to skip out as often as you can. I've had two who made me wish I had school on Saturday. I've been lucky. Some kids never find teachers like that. Some bring you lots of things to work with; others make you stay in your seat and fill in blanks and memorize stuff. Those teachers are stinky. They say stinky words, give you stinky looks, and grade you on stinky report cards. Some teachers are great. Like I said, I had two like that. They put bandages on my hurts—on my heart, on my mind, on my spirit. Those teachers cared about me and let me know it. They gave me wings.

Today's Education. Used with permission.

The following essay on "Cats and People" was turned in by an astute pupil:

"Cats and people are funny animals. Cats have four paws but only one ma. People have forefathers and only one mother.

"When a cat smells a rat he gets excited; so do people.

"Cats carry tails, and a lot of people carry tales, too.

"All cats have fur coats. Some people have fur coats, and the ones who don't have fur coats say catty things about the ones who have them."

—Unknown

Drivers should try to remember not to drive too close apart.

My absolutional opinion is bad walkers such as jay walkers should be given tickets just like bad drivers. It is for their own safeness.

People should not get behind the steering wheel until they have practiced driving for at least a month.

Hygiene is to keep healthy on the inside while safety is to keep healthy on the outside.

Scurry is a disease caused by driving too fast.

People should not try to drive when they are ready to drop from pure exhausteration.

One good safety rule we learned on our last vacation trip was don't let the car get so rambled from lack of unkeep.

Beginning last month, we have not been having to pay anything for our gas at the filling station. They just take daddy's motorized signature and then we just drive off.

On our last vacation trip, one of my idiot brothers (that will remain nameless) kept squirming on the front seat until he was finally renegaded to the back seat.

Safety is not playing tag in the car.

Safety is politeness. It is to act on the road like you talk when you say thank you and your welcome.

Safety is to help the driver by politely keeping shut up.

Safety is what saves iodine.

Safety is everybody on the highway acting like good samericans.

Safety is not being on the same spot that a car is on.

Safety is a revolution to keep around the year.

Nationwide Mutual Insurance Company, Minutes

What's education all about? Several years ago Jerry Simpson decided to ask those who should know—the kids in class. He queried pupils in six public elementary schools of Waynesboro, Virginia. Their unedited answers to questions about various aspects of schools and education convinced him that, despite "meaningful dialogues" between educators, the ones who really have the say on education are the pupils. Here are some of their replies:

A teacher is a educated person who is to help other people. She does not go to school for her own good.

Education is when your parents make you go to bed at 9:30 and get up at 7 to go to school. When you get home your mother asks you what you learned, and you say "nothing," then you have to go to bed at 9:30 again.

Education learns you how to do things. You go to learn so that you will have some more marbles in your head.

Education is when someone is engaged.

A school board is something that bosses a princeable around.

I don't know much about the school board, in fact I don't know anything about it, so I really can't tell you much about it, but I can tell you one thing. It has done good work.

A principal is a person that is a member of the school board. He tells the teachers what they can do and where they can go.

A principal is someone who doesn't trust the intercom, you know, because he is always shouting, "Testing, one, two, three."

I think a PTA is a meeting where you have to wait around a lot.

A PTA is on Monday once every month. It is mostly for parents, but children can come and sit and be bored.

A PTA is something like a woman's meeting. They talk a little while then everybody goes to have refreshments.

A school teaches you stuff. You learn how to read and write. And people won't go around calling you a dumb head then.

I think a school is a place where I belong at.

—Jerry H. Simpson, Jr. Education Reporter,
.Waynesboro, Virginia, *Today's Education.* Used with permission.

A law school professor was puzzled about the mark he should give the student who wrote about wills:

"A will is a written document in which a person tells how he wants his property divided among his errors."

Elberton (Georgia) *Star*

Patrick Henry was not a very bright boy. He had blue eyes and brown hair. He got married, and then said, "Give me liberty, or give me death."

—Unknown

One young fellow was more astute than he realized when he wrote: "The world is a big ball which revolves on its taxes."

—Unknown

A sixth grader wrote: "To prevent head colds, use an agonizer to spray nose until it drops into your throat."

Colorado School Journal

Until the teacher can finally clear things up for him, the elementary school youngster's mind seems to be a vast storehouse of miscellaneous misinformation—part true, part false and wholly delightful. Below are some examples I've gleaned from music test papers and essays through the years:

"Handel was half German, half Italian and half English. He was rather large."

"Music sung by two people at the same time is called a duel."

"Morris dancing is a country survival from the time when people were happy."

"The only fugue I can think of is the one between the Hatfields and the McCoys."

Quote

A little girl who lived in a wealthy suburb was asked to write a story about a poor family and she began, "This family was very poor. The mommy was poor. The daddy was poor. The brothers and sisters were poor. The maid was poor. The nurse was poor. The butler was poor. The cook was poor. The yardman was poor. . . ."

—Bob Talbert, Columbia State

A small boy was asked to write an essay in as few words as possible on two of life's greatest problems. He wrote: "Twins."

—*Sunshine Magazine*

A teacher told her class to write a four-line verse that showed action. One boy wrote:

> A boy walked down a railroad track,
> A train was coming fast;
> The boy jumped off the railroad track
> To let the train go past.

The teacher said the verse did not show enough action, so the boy revised it as follows:

> A boy walked down a railroad track,
> A train was coming fast;
> The train jumped off the railroad track
> To let the boy go past."

Sunshine Magazine

Selections from book reports: "I recommend this book to anyone who likes to read about prestork life." . . . *Mutiny on the Bounty* was all about Dick and Jane and their dog spot. It really wasn't but I don't think you read these book reports." . . . *"To Kill a Mockingbird* was about Gregory Peck being a lawyer in the South. It was one of the books I've watched."

—*Today's Catholic Teacher, Education Digest*

Once there was a cat who never wanted to do anything for himself. So he asked other animals smaller than him to do his work. He would beat them up if they started any trouble. They did all of his work for him. If he wanted something to eat he would send them one by one until he got it. Then one day a fox came along and said, "Stop picking on those poor little animals." The cat told him to mind his business. The fox said, "You know I am right." They started fighting and fighting until the cat was dead. The fox said to the other animals, "You won't be bossed around anymore." Moral: A good thing doesn't last forever.

—The Rotarian

Once I had a dream, do you know what I dreamt? Well, I will tell you.

My cousin and I went to this school, and nobody was there. So we amused ourselves by going in the art room. And we made a giant balloon and we wove a basket out of straw. We attached the balloon and the basket with string. We brought it out of the art room. We cut a hole in the roof and nailed nails in the floor and tied string to the nails and attached the string to the balloon and I got in and by accident my cousin cut the string and I flew up in the sky and my mother and cousin flew up with me and a jet plain went zoom! There was a hole in the balloon and we went right down and landed in the tires.

When we got settled down we had a picnic in the tires and suddenly a blue elephant came smash in our lunch.

—Serena Collison, age 7, Republic of China,
The Rotarian

Teacher Anne M. Bailey of Pullman, Washington, sends a language arts paper in which eight-year-old Carl Ott interprets to parents "How Children Feel":

"Some parents don't give children rights. No right to go in the company living room, no right to wrestle in the recreation room, no right to stay up late. You want your children to follow your rules but they would be happier if they had rights. But don't give us to many rights or we'll be spoiled. Don't make us spoiled and don't make us rightless.

"Children like to be wanted. Like if there is three children and a father and mother in a family—two children are talking, mother and father are talking. Let the littlest one get into the confortha-tion. It can talk just as well as anyone. It feels not wanted, in the middle of nowhere. Why don't you take him on your lap. Children have feelings. They can be hurt easily.

"Children like to have fun—they get board. Say some day they have played with all their toys. They don't have any money to go downtown. Don't say, 'Oh, you have so many toys you forgot about all of them.'Can't you suggest a few games? They may not like it, but at least you can say you helped. You can even loan them some money. They'ed love that.

"When the country fair is coming, the children are getin excited. A good way to quiet them down is, every night give them their favorite food. When they run toward some ride at the fair, don't emberis them in front of everybody by telling him to either behave or you will send him back to the car.

"Children don't like to just look at a thing and leave. They like to go over things twice. Don't hurry them. They may never see the place again. They can't own a camera yet so they like to get things on their memory by looking again and again. They try very hard to please you most of the time. So please them and don't rush them."

NEA Journal, April, 1964.
(Now *Today's Education.*) Used with permission.

Children sometimes write with more human interest than they speak. Witness this rough draft of an essay on "Communication" by a Ridgewood, New Jersey, fourth grader, sent to us by superintendent Lloyd W. Ashby:

"Communicate is to get ideas across. People communicate by writing letters too. Here is a typical story of a housewife communicating. One day a young housewife was very ergent to tell her father something. Things had been going funny, so she had gone to the dockter's. And to her surprise, she was pragne. There are many ways she could tell him but she wanted to do it the fast way, by telephone. When she called her father who was a long way off, he was very happy for her. This is one of the many way's communication helps the world."

~ *NEA Journal,* April, 1964. (Now *Today's Education.*) Used with permission.

Eighth grader Becky Schlemmer submits a manuscript, "My Dad is a Teacher," in which she states:

"I'm real proud of my dad, even if he is a teacher. Kids who don't know any better think a teacher for a father must be just awful. True, he is a busy man (Watching TV, taking a nap, reading the papers). But most of the time I forget that he even is a teacher. The best part is that my teachers don't expect me to be a straight-A student just because my dad is a brain.

"Teachers are very original in what they say, particularly

outside the classroom. It's fun to listen to teachers gad away at teachers' picnics. Who would guess that these joking, gossiping people are those same wise brains in the classroom?

"Teachers' salaries are nothing to brag about. But all the salaries in the world couldn't make up for the fact that my dad is a teacher."

> *NEA Journal,* April, 1964. (Now *Today's Education*.) Used with permission.

. . . But the curtain of confusion extends all the way out to Palo Alto, California, where teacher Cynthia Diamond tells us about a student who was asked to list the characteristics of America's early frontiersmen. He wrote: "Courageous, strong, and full of wandering lust."

> Unknown

TEACHING MATERIALS—BOOKS

A new aid to rapid—almost magical—learning has made its appearance. Indications are that if it catches on, all the electronic gadgets will be so much junk. The new device is known as Built-in Orderly Organized Knowledge. The makers generally call it by its initials, BOOK.

Many advantages are claimed over the old-style learning and teaching aids on which most people are brought up nowadays. . . . It is made entirely without mechanical parts to go wrong or need replacement.

Anyone can use BOOK, even children, and it fits comfortably into the hands. . . .

How does this revolutionary, unbelievably easy invention work? Basically BOOK consists only of a large number of paper sheets. These may run to hundreds where BOOK covers a lengthy program of information. . . . Each sheet of paper presents the user with an information sequence in the form of symbols. . . . No buttons need to be pressed to move from one sheet to another, to open or close BOOK, or to start it working.

BOOK may be taken up at any time and used by merely

opening it. Instantly it is ready to use. . . . The user may turn at will to any sheet, going backwards or forwards as he pleases. . . .

Quote

A classic is something they give away free in order to get a person to join a book club.

Chicago Sun-Times

See the book. Isn't the book pretty? It is blue. It is a pro-fess-ion-al book. It would be good for teachers to read. I am not going to read it. I am going to read *Life*. It has pretty pictures in it. There are funny stories in it. I make my pupils read ser-i-ous books. They are dopes, isn't that a scream?

—Unknown

TEACHERS' MEETINGS

Some of our teachers have been spending time at the beach, yelling at the waves in order to be inured to getting no response when school opens.

—Bill Copeland, *Sarasota Journal*

A conference is a gathering of important people who singly can do nothing, but together can decide that nothing can be done.

—*Sunshine Magazine*

TEACHERS AND TEACHING

When a teacher who had been in the city school system for more than 50 years retired, a big party was given in her honor. Afterward, a former pupil offered to escort her home, but she insisted on going alone. "Mrs. Brown, aren't you afraid to be out so late by yourself?" he asked.

"What's there to be afraid of?" she retorted. "I've whipped every man in town!"

—Angeline W. Baxter (Nashville, Tennessee)

The young nursery school teacher was complaining about how

hard she works: "Do you know what time I get up? When the big hand is on 12 and the little hand is on 5."

Miami Tribune, Comedy and Comment

Describing her first day back in grade school after a long absence, a teacher said, "It was like trying to hold 35 corks under water at the same time."

American Salesman, Quote

When in the latest fashion
So attractively you're dressed
Won't you try some exercises
As just a little test?
Stand before your mirror
Full-length upon the wall.
Turn around, bend over,
As if picking up a ball.
(Are garters glaring back at you?
Stocking tops and flesh?
Remember, children's thoughts
Can easily digress).
Next reach high into the air
As on the chalkboard you write
Ask someone who's watching
Exactly what's in sight.
(Will small folks on lower chairs
Get quite a different view?
Is it Playtex they are seeing
When they are watching you?)
Now sit before your mirror
And try a pose or two,
Like crossing right leg over left,
As we are prone to do.
You may be teaching something
That needs some careful thought;
But perhaps it's difficult
To tell what they've been taught.
While keeping up with fashion
Remember in the end
It's little things that really count,
Like how to sit and bend.

—Unknown

Some teachers have a secret code. If you chance to observe two teachers meet and pass in the hall, and one exclaims, "HIF," that means "Hurray, it's Friday!"

But if one says to the other, "MGIM," that means, "My gosh, it's Monday."

—Unknown

She had graduated from college and, despite the fact that she had had no instruction in how to teach, was put in charge of the first grade. Not a word was heard from her for two days, but at the end of that time, she burst into the principal's office.

"I quit," she exclaimed. "There isn't a single brat in that whole room who knows how to read."

Rotary Reel

The faculty committee was organizing the order of examinations. It was decided that the harder subjects should be placed first in the list and that history should have the final place. The lady teacher of history protested stoutly:

"But," declared the chairman," it most certainly is one of the easiest subjects."

With an air of resoluteness, the young lady shook her head and announced firmly, "Not the way I teach it. Indeed, according to the methods I use, it is a most difficult study and extremely perplexing."

—Unknown

> The better the teacher, the fairer the grade,
> So therefore an interesting point can be made:
> It seems only right (and a fabulous thought)
> For pupils to mark on how teachers have taught.

—Elinor K. Rose

Fables for Teachers

In seems that a grasshopper became concerned about the future when the summer was punctured by the advent of frosty weather. He had stored no food and had no snug home for the winter. In some concern he went to his friends, the ants, and requested sanctuary for the winter season. The ants were sympathetic but unobliging. They suggested, since they had no space or supplies to spare, that the grasshopper take his problem to the nearby university. "A first-rate mental institution," said the ants, "which deals with all the problems of mankind."

The grasshopper, grateful for the suggestion, hopped in to see the university president. After listening attentively to the grasshopper's tale of woe, he sent him hopping to the home economics department, since it appeared that the problem was basically a nutritional one. The head of the home economics department, after hearing the story, felt that the problem was really a matter of supply and demand and could more properly be dealt with by the economists in the social science department.

Even the economists were baffled by this problem, and, as a last resort, and in complete desperation, they suggested that perhaps the workshop being held in the College of Education might offer some help, since "they could handle *any* kind of problem." Here the 'hopper found a warm, friendly group atmosphere. His problem was taken under serious advisement, out of which emerged the recommendation that he become a mole for the winter, live in an underground burrow, and diet on roots and worms.

Happily convinced that his problem was solved, the grasshopper skipped merrily down the road in the frosty twilight until—horrors—it dawned on him that he had not been instructed in the art of becoming a mole. Back he came, just as the workshop director was packing up his materials until the following summer.

"Oh, sir," chirped the grasshopper, "I did forget to ask you one question. How do I become a mole?"

There was a long silence, broken only by muted nibblings as the director worried a ragged fingernail. At last he spoke, "Didn't you know, old boy, that we workshoppers are concerned only with the basic principles? You will have to work out the details."

—Anonymous

The Poor Teacher's Soliloquy

I'm trying very hard to be a good teacher, but my principal says I just don't have what it takes.

He says I can't keep the noise down in my room. I guess we did make some noise the other day when the class was studying the effect of exercise on the pulse rate. The students jumped about a bit, but they couldn't see how to exercise by sitting in their seats. I wish my room were not right over the principal's office.

The principal says I'm always entertaining students with films and other things, like last week when we projected the photographs of our visit to the airport weather station and played the tape recordings of our interviews with the meteorologists. Probably the trip to the airport was too much fun too.

The principal says my students are always arguing. But they just can't seem to agree on some things—at least not at the beginning. Last Monday they really became steamed up over the issue of halting the tests of nuclear weapons. Even George, who usually doesn't recite much, got into the act.

The principal claims I have favorites among my students. He says John and Pete should do the same work as the others instead of getting to build a Geiger counter. I guess I was a soft touch when they talked me out of doing the experiments on bar magnets. They said they had already performed them some years ago in Pete's basement lab. You know, Pete has more apparatus in his laboratory than we do in the school.

The principal says I must be lazy because I don't keep a class chart at the front of the room with students' exam grades on it. He says I'm overlooking a good means of motivating my students. It's not that I'm lazy, but I just don't seem to have time for the chart—what with the students always telling me about the science projects they are doing.

Above all, says the principal, my room is untidy—always cluttered with books and magazines.

> —William C. Odell. Used with permission of the
> Association of Childhood Education International,
> Washington, D.C.

The Fable of the Eraser-Clapper

There once was a red one-room school house filled with children.

As commonly happens in one-room schools, they were learning to play and live together as all children do. Nothing was unusual about this school except the social strata that began to develop as a result of being a one-room school.

The children soon began to see that on the social ladder, the flag putter-upper and the chalkboard washer ranked very near the top along with eraser clapper. The lower strata consisted of (in order) the floor sweeper, water-pail filler, and with the wood bringer-inner, and the toilet-paper replacer (for the outhouse) being far behind in last place.

It developed, as the school year went on, that the student who was mischievous and questioning became the wood bringer-inner and the toilet-paper replacer and the "good" student who always behaved himself (almost always were the girls because the boys played too rough when they played "King of the Hill") became the chalkboard washer and the eraser clapper.

And it followed that when the report cards went home, the eraser clappers got A's and the floor sweepers and toilet paper replacers got the D's and F's. This was the beginning of merit pay.

L.A. Paffenroth

The local school has gone in for team teaching. That's where the teachers gang up so no one can be held responsible.

—Changing Times

In the good old fashioned school days,
    days of the golden rule,
Teacher said, "Good morning! class,"
    and so she started school.
Alas! How different things are now,
    the school day can't begin
Til someone finds the socket
    and plugs the teacher in.

—Unknown

What is a teacher? Here's one pupil's assessment: A teacher is someone who stands right smack in front of the problem, erases the board before you get a chance to see it and then wonders why you don't understand it.

Maryland Teacher, Quote

There are three things to remember when teaching school: Know your stuff, know whom you are stuffing, and then stuff them elegantly.

—Lola May, *Education Digest*

Two teachers were talking after a PTA meeting when one said, "I prefer to teach in an elementary school so I'll have a place to park."

—Unknown

We hope all teachers will enjoy the summer and not worry about being automated out of work. They'll still be needed for playground duty, fire drills, collecting milk money and PTA.

—Unknown

Teachers have tough problems. One moment they're told to worry about too many overcrowded schools, and in the next breath they're told to worry about too many dropouts.

Nathan Nielsen, Comedy and Comment

Pedro was selling papers at a downtown corner, shouting "Extra! Extra! Two teachers swindled!" A local teacher walked by and after hearing the headlines bought a paper.

She hastily glanced through the paper and said, "Hey, there's nothing here about a swindle."

"Extra! Extra!" shouted Pedro, "Three teachers swindled."

Laugh Book

The teacher, after dictating the sentence "The beaver eats bark and twigs" to her grade five class, made the mistake of checking their books, and discovered that one pupil had written "The beaver eats bark and two eggs." Then she had a complete mental breakdown.

—Toronto Education Quarterly,
published by the Toronto Board of Education

A teacher who insists she will draw and quarter us if we reveal her name says the principal of her school told a funny at a faculty meeting the other day. "Well," she sighed, "anyway, since he is the principal we all laughed as if it were funny."

Seems a teacher (so the principal's story went) boarded a bus and was busy doing some of her own homework on geography when a man who evidently had spent the day in a tavern boarded and sat down beside her.

The teacher's geography book, on her lap, fell open at a map of South America and the tipsy man happened to notice. He studied the map for several seconds, then mumbled:

"Damn! I'm on the wrong bus again."

—Roger Devlin,
Tulsa Tribune, Comedy and Comment

There's satellites, rockets and electrical sockets,
New germs to uncover and stars to discover;
A trip to the moon is enticing and might be;
Living on Mars is entirely likely.
Obsessed with the technical whirl they call progress,
I'm literally batty but must not regress;

Evolution, I love thee, but you're hard on the creatures
Who keep up with your pace, the poor science teachers.
                    —J.T., *Passing Marks,* San Bernardino City Schools

A teacher's life is filled with troubles,
Squirt guns, spitballs, gum that bubbles,
Whispers, notes, and comic books,
Apple-polishers, dirty looks;
Spring with its resultant fever;
Earnest workers, gay deceivers;
Homework papers overdue,
Recitations and review;
Grades, with the complaints they bring,
Bells that regularly ring;
Youth that always keeps its bloom,
Laughter filling up the room.
And though I speak with indiscretion—
I'm glad I chose this mad profession!

                                        —Unknown

My teacher is mad, my teacher is sad
Because the children act so bad.
The pencil she fly, the ink won't dry
And then my teacher start to cry.

                                        —Unknown

The new elementary school teacher, with the ink on her diploma barely dry, threw herself enthusiastically into her first teaching assignment.

She was elated when she saw the list of students in her class, with each student's name followed by a number—Johnny Jones, 145; Mary Long, 148; Christopher Moore, 150; and so forth.

When the principal stopped in and asked her how things were going, she replied, "Oh, wonderful. How else could they be when I have such an intelligent class."

She held up the list and said, "Just look at their IQ's!"

She was quickly deflated when the principal said, "Those numbers aren't their IQ's—those are their locker numbers."

                    Council Bluffs Nonpareil, Comedy and Comment

The teacher asked Perry to tell her what a hypocrite is. Replied Perry, "It's a boy who comes to school with a smile on his face."

                                        —Unknown

The Bloomington, Illinois, *Pantagraph,* tells about a little kid so tough the teacher keeps bringing him apples.

Comedy and Comment

One superintendent included in his evaluation of a former teacher these words: "Mr. Nye not only kept abreast of the latest developments in his teaching field, but he also managed to get along splendidly with me—no small accomplishment according to my secretary."

—Unknown

Letters of Reference:

—This teacher has talents but has kept them well hidden.

—His leadership is outstanding except for his lack of ability to get along with subordinates.

—Open to suggestions but never follows same.

—Is keenly analytical and his highly developed mentality could best be utilized in the research and development field. He lacks common sense.

—Never makes the same mistake twice but it seems to me he has made them all once.

—Such time as she can spare from adornment of her person, she devotes to the neglect of her profession.

—Unknown

Sign in teacher placement office: "Don't underestimate yourself. Let us do it for you."

—*Scandal Sheet,* Graham (Tex.) Rotary Club,
Quote

A teacher being interviewed for a job in a modern junior high school with a dynamic curriculum was asked if she had previously taught at the secondary level.

"Certainly."

"In junior high school?"

"Yes."

"In grade eight?"

"Yes."

"Block-of-time method?"

"Yes."

"Integration of subject matter in the block-of-time in grade eight?"

"No, no integration of subject matter."

"Sorry, we need a specialist."

                                              —Unknown

The mayor met the principal of the toughest school in town. The principal was obviously downcast, and the mayor asked him why.

"School's been open only a short time," the educator explained, "and already we've had 39 dropouts."

"Is that so bad?" the mayor said. "After all, you're in the roughest section of town."

"That's the trouble," replied the principal, "38 of the 39 dropouts were teachers."

                          —James Shurlock, *Family Weekly, Quote*

Two English teachers, spending their summer vacation traveling, stopped in a small Texas town for lunch. One of them noticed a cowhand walking a few feet ahead of them and whispered, "Look! A bowlegged cowboy."

"Isn't there a more tactful way to say it?" the other teacher said. "I'm sure if our beloved Shakespeare were alive he could express it more poetically."

For a few moments the first teacher was silent. Then she said aloud, "Look ho, there goes a man with parentheses for legs."

                                        Sunshine Magazine

She's an expert with projectors, flicking switches, changing reels; here, mechanical adeptness she outstandingly reveals. She can run the duplicator, she can type just like a pro; give advice on many subjects—she's a teacher, don't you know?

Sometimes she's a stern policeman, grimly laying down the law, making all her little cherubs look at her with trembling awe. She's an amateur detective, shrewdly sleuthing childish pranks; as a salesman for insurance she could easily top the ranks.

She's an office secretary, keeping records, books, reports; you should see her on the playground as she supervises sports. Bloody noses don't upset her, neither childish quarrels nor noise; she's a friend of all the parents with her tactful charm and poise.

You should see her pet collection—hamsters, baby mice, and snakes, guppies, turtles, snails, and lizards, goldfish, too, for goodness' sakes! Yes, they tell me she's a teacher, helping youthful minds to climb up the steep ascent of knowledge. Tell me how she finds the time!

Sunshine Magazine

He abhors the word teacher, and calls himself a "catalectic provocateur."

—Unknown

I'll never forget my first day of teaching. I prepared a seating chart, alphabetically. In the front row were Fannie Browning and Fannie Bock, and I commented, "Well, what do you know, two fannies in the front row."

—M. Dale Baughman

On "Who Do You Trust?", ABC-TV network show, the interviewer Woody Woodbury asked a "Bunny Mother," who hires, trains and supervises Bunnies for the Playboy Clubs, what requisites the girls need to qualify. "They must be natural and unaffected beauties," she replied. To illustrate her point she told of rejecting three candidates that day; one was too bosomy, one had a hairdo that was too bouffant, and the third wore padding on her hips.

Woody pondered for a moment, then quipped, "In other words, today you turned down Flopsy, Mopsy and Cottontail."

Reader's Digest

I remarked to a young superintendent in my office seeking a teacher of girls' physical education, "The school who gets this young lady will get a prize."

Quick as a flash, the young executive shot back, "May I see it, please?"

—M. Dale Baughman

A college administrative officer, at a loss what to say in a letter of recommendation concerning a doubtful applicant, finally wrote: "When you come to know the applicant as we know him, you will come to appreciate him as we appreciate him."

Mississippi Educational Advance

I write you in support of the application of Miss Jones, who is looking for a position which offers more money and less work. Miss Jones is an attractive young lady with unusual social graces and financial acumen of a high order. She plays the accordion with grace and speed. I personally picked her as a teacher and my batting average as a picker is very good—more than 25%—which is considerably higher than that of my predecessor. Miss Jones has many virtues; her only fault lies in her inability to teach school.

                                                              —Unknown

Teacher Recommendations:

This teacher has skills and techniques but manages never to use them.
—Her self-expression is laudable. With great facility she can express a single thought in a term paper at the drop of a hat.
—Needs skillful supervision since he approaches brilliancy.
—Attentive, always listens well, receptive to advice but never heeds same.
—Has a keen mind with analytical acumen; his highly developed intellect would serve him well in basic research. He has common sense in small measure.

────────────── **VOCABULARY—WORDS** ──────────────

"The Clifton Forge Rescue Squad was called to Iron Gate for Clarence Milton, Jr., seven, who had a possible broken leg. The squad splintered his leg and removed him to the C & O Hospital."
                                    --*Clifton Forge* (Virginia) *Review*

Letter left on a teacher's desk:

Dear Teacher:

I try to keep calm and collected whenever you tell us that nouns are inflected; I know that your smiles tend to fade into frowns when I always add s to form plurals of nouns. I'm right when I do it with truths and with houses, but wrong when I do it with tooths and with mouses. You applaud when I write of beliefs and of chiefs, but you groan when I follow the rule and write thiefs. If the plural of man should be written as men, then why isn't more than one can written cen? You can tell us that goose has the plural of geese, but moose and papoose don't give meese and papeese, yet I'm right when I just add an s to write nooses, and mongoose in the plural is written mongooses. You've told us that English is changing each year—here's a change for our nouns that I now volunteer: It will lift from us pupils much strain and much stress if we pluralize always by just adding s. So from now on, dear teacher, I'm flouting the rules, and I hope my reform is adopted by schools. I'll be writing mans, womans, deers, oxs, and knifes, leafs, milks, sheeps, mouses, foots, matchs, wifes. So that childs will be happier all of their lifes.

—J.E. Parsons, reprinted from the
Toronto Education Quarterly,
published by the Toronto Board of Education.

Teacher: "Construct a sentence using the word exchange."

Student: "The frequency of absorbable radiation depends upon the elastic constant of the molecule and the process of energy exchange is therefore in accord with the equipartition theory."

—Unknown

A philologist says that nine words account for a fourth of all that we say or write. They are *and, be, have, it, of, the, will, I* and *you.* In fact, these nine, with an additional 34 words, account for half our literary work. The 34 words are: *about, all, as, at, but, can, come, day, dear, for, get, go, hear, her, if, in, me, much, not, no, one, say, she, so, that, there, they, this, time, though, we, with, write,* and *your.*

Because they get tired of looking at and speaking all these one-syllable words, professional men have to spice their literary product with such words as proliferation, disestablishment, obfuscation and ophthalmologist.

—Unknown

Dick and Jane are dead. Chalk will henceforth be known as an intra-digital calcifrictator. And the principal will be called the resource transfer co-ordinator. Using this vein of redefinition a student becomes a resource retriever while the school year is called an academic chronophase.

These phrases are part of the semantic feedback now going into Ontario schools as a result of hundreds of seminars, papers and reports digested by 10,000 Ontario teachers who converged on Toronto during the March winter holiday.

Somewhat dumbfounded, teachers heard that, in the schools of the future, they will be known as "resource agents." Those who did not despair responded with poetic vigor to the novel nomenclature and began a fast-spreading game of changing the common terms of today into the terminology of the future.

On the threshold of a vast movement to re-define the role of teacher, nervous academicians have channeled their jitters into witticism. Here is a list—sorry, a variative random compendium—of slightly exaggerated but quasi-credible appellations as overheard and/or invented in teachers' lounges:

Art: Psycho-sublimic video-spasmodics	New Math: Neo-systematic computology
Ballpoint Pen: Permo-synthetic communicator	Pencil: Ligno-graphitic communicator
Bell: Audio-temporal stimu-lator	Period: Investigation unit
Blackboard: Calcigraphic mediator	School: Resource transfer center
Book: Video-verbal resource	School Year: Academic chrono-phase
Chair: Osteo-plastic form receptor	Student: Resource retriever
Classroom: Resource environ-ment	Subject: Investigation area
Crayon: Polychromatic com-municator	Washroom: Hydro-hygenic facilitator
	Waste Basket: Rejectacle
	Window: Perspectum exter-ializer

—Unknown

Really now, things could be worse—have been—and are. When we get 180-degree turns in words the tyranny is upon us. In less than one generation the supposed antonyms of "hot" and "cool" assumed a common meaning for approved life-style.

Words and language limit and control our lives. Therefore, when such words as "square," "industrious," "frugal," "obedient" and "diligent" drift far off course with meanings of dubious praise, we are shaken up under the tyranny of words. But language is forever changing, and who are we to stem the tide?

Nedra Newkirk Lamar says that no matter how much we are grateful and thankful for the English language, we simply can't trust it. At one time or another some teacher told us that *er* endings on words meant somebody or something who does something. A trapper is one who traps, a player is one who plays. It follows that a shoulder is one who "shoulds" and a finger is somebody or something that "fings." Fing, fang, fung—get it? No, you can't trust it.

It isn't very kind to foreigners, either; too many meanings for words—these two for example, "fit" and "plug." There are at least seven common meanings for each.

Someone said that there are 850 basic words while the total number of different words has been estimated at 450,000.

If what Disraeli wrote is true, "With words we govern men," then building word power is a meaningful goal, in which case only some people are tyrannized by words, the governed.

Aren't words wonderful and tyrannizing? They give us the young labor leader telling a bedtime story to his son, "Once upon a time and a half . . . " and how about a Lawrence Welk fan counting with his five-year-old son,"A-one, a-two, a-three."

A Californian says he's still a little nervous about the public-address announcement he heard at the San Francisco airport concerning his plane for Los Angeles. "Flight 608," the voice intoned solemnly, "is now ready for its final departure."

Editors of a recent college edition of the Random House Dictionary say it was necessary to add 7,000 new words to keep abreast of the changing English language.

What they ought to do now in concert with other publishers is declare a moratorium on new words until people learn how to spell more of the old ones.

Radar spelled backwards is radar; they've got you coming and going.

—M. Dale Baughman, *Contemporary Education*

Index